Critics' Praise for
Cambodia: A Book for People Who Find Television Too Slow

"Fawcett is a purely intellectual guerilla who has declared war on what he calls the "Global Village" . . . He is also a man obsessed with the agonies of the Cambodian people at the hands of the Khmer Rouge . . . The heart and soul of *Cambodia* is its subtext—a thoughtful, well-informed and provocative examination of the linkages between the atrocities of colonialism in the Belgian Congo (as contemplated by Joseph Conrad and Hannah Arendt), the more recent acts of genocide by the Khmer Rouge, and the crimes against humanity that are embodied in the Global Village. He concludes with a ringing call for a blow against the Global Village—and a kind of self-liberation—through the very acts of remembering and imagining."

—Jonathan Kirsch, *Los Angeles Times*

"A set of cunning skirmishes in an all-out attack on the automatisms of modern life . . . exhilarating, silly and insightful, grumpy and affectionate. Kind of like modern life."—*Kirkus*

"This extraordinary book defies categorization . . . a warning against global genocide by developers, a critical discussion of the late twentieth-century novel, and a heartbreaking study of genocide. Thirteen experimental, often hilarious stories are combined with a long essay on the slaughter of millions of innocent Cambodians by the Khmer Rouge; each page displays both story and essay, inviting the reader to jump between them . . . Like Marlow in Conrad's *Heart of Darkness*, the narrator is haunted to madness by the horrors he has observed . . . *Cambodia* cannot be ignored: its technique is dazzling, and its grim message reminds us of the presence of evil in our time."—*Booklist*

"A guerilla for literacy, Fawcett is passionate, articulate, and intelligent. A fascinating book."—*Toronto Globe and Mail*

CAMBODIA:
A Book for People Who Find Television Too Slow

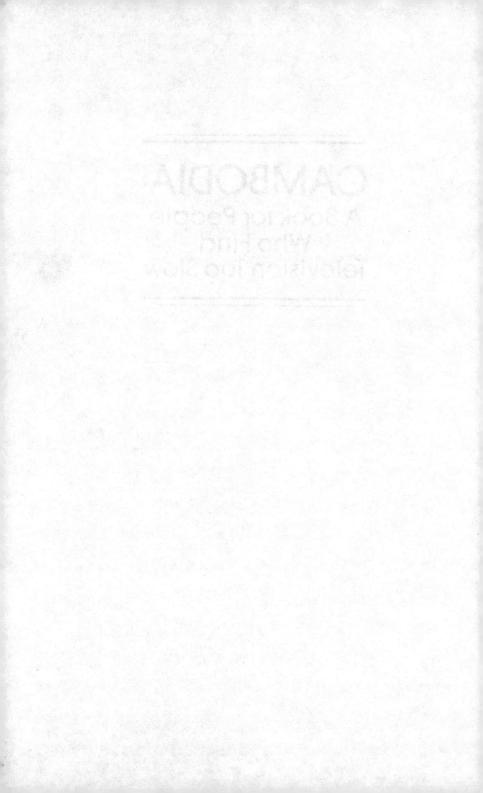

CAMBODIA:
A Book for People Who Find Television Too Slow

Brian Fawcett

Collier Books
Macmillan Publishing Company
New York

First published by Talonbooks in Canada, first U.S. edition by Grove Press, 1988. This paperback edition is reprinted by arrangement with Grove Press, a division of Wheatland Corporation.

"The Fat Family Goes to the World's Fair" is dedicated to the memory of Howard Broomfield (1946–1986)

Collier Books
Macmillan Publishing Company
866 Third Avenue, New York, NY 10022

Library of Congress Cataloging-in-Publication Data
Fawcett, Brian, 1944–
    Cambodia : a book for people who find television too slow / Brian
Fawcett.—1st Collier Books ed.
        p. cm.
    ISBN 0-02-032150-3
    I. Title.
PR9199.3.F39C25   1989   89-9878   CIP
813'.54—dc20

Cover by Javier Romero Design © 1989

First Collier Books Edition 1989

10   9   8   7   6   5   4   3   2   1

Printed in the United States of America

for Nancy

Preface

The intellectual and cultural proposition underlying much of contemporary artistic theory and practice is that reality in art is secured by subtexts that trail meanings in all directions—into material existence and its procedures and institutions, into language, and into moral philosophy, theology and the natural and social sciences. These subtexts, almost never explicit, are believed to be accessible to the cognoscenti if not always to the general public.

The formal method of this book argues against that proposition. First of all, there is no evidence that *anyone* in this atomized world culture adequately understands its subtexts and/or the reference networks they are grounded in. Second, even if the subtexts were comprehended, to create art based on exclusionary subtexts is dangerously antidemocratic. There is a great deal of evidence to indicate that contemporary artistic theory and practice, like its telecommunications and information equivalents, discourages and disables political, social, artistic and intellectual discourse for the general public. The result is that those forms of discourse are disappearing from the public realm across Western civilization, and are becoming the intellectual property of a new kind of privileged class.

In response to a conviction that widely comprehended discourse is fundamental to democratic institutions, I have made the subtext of this book visible and literal to the best of my ability.

Contents

Contents

CAMBODIA:
A Book for People
Who Find
Television Too Slow

On the Difficulties of Crowd Control

On a sunny morning at Kent State University in Kent, Ohio, militiamen of the Ohio National Guard open fire on a crowd of students protesting the invasion of Cambodia by American troops five days before. By the time the guardsmen stop firing their weapons, four students are dead and nine more are wounded. The date is May 4th, 1970.

It happens that a television crew from one of the local stations is present at the scene, and within hours the footage the crew shoots of the incident is being broadcast on nearly every television station in North America. The camerawork isn't the sort that wins prizes, but it has a peculiar spontaneity about it, perhaps because the shootings were as much a surprise to the cameramen as they were to the demonstrating students.

The public outcry over the next several days is loud, long and indignant: these innocent, brave students are victims of outright murder. They are Americans, after all, exercising their God-given right to freedom of expression. Such atrocities of authority should not be possible in the United States of America.

1

We think we know what went on in Cambodia. An article has now appeared in *National Geographic*, with photographs of the piles of whitening skulls fouling the rice paddies, and the walls covered with photographs of some of those who were tortured, made to write confessions and then killed—along with their families—because they could read and write, wore glasses, spoke foreign languages or erred in their interpretation of Khmer Rouge doctrine.

Most of the victims of the Khmer Rouge were killed merely because they could remember a different kind of world than the one the Khmer Rouge were attempting to recreate out of the rubble of the Vietnam

Eventually the furore dies down without a clear public assignation of who or what was responsible. Later, cynics will note that the four Kent State killings cause the virtual collapse of the American student movement as a tool for social change. Real life, they sneer, has visited itself upon the theoretical realities of academia—a little napalm found out what the student movement is really made of.

It is true that after the incident there are fewer campus protests by students, and that when protests take place, the crowds are smaller and much more wary. But while that may be true, it is also true that the movement to stop the undeclared war in Vietnam and Cambodia, in which students form at least a substantial part of the front line, has succeeded in hamstringing American military ambitions in Southeast Asia, probably to the point of preventing the use of "tactical" nuclear weapons there. Others will say it was Watergate and the general indecision created by the revelations of Presidential lying and corruption that ultimately force the American withdrawal from Southeast Asia.

All such speculations, however, are now antiquarian. It all happened a long time ago. And who really cares? Ask your best friend or your spouse how many students died at Kent State, and why. Few will remember the details. The students, they will muse, must have had reasons for being out there that day. Maybe it was a nice day for a protest march against the Fascist authorities. The National Guardsmen likewise: bullets in their

---

War. Others were killed because they imagined a different kind of world. Memory and imagination were both capital offences in Khmer Rouge Cambodia.

Statistical estimates of the number of people who died are unreliable and they will remain so. Statistics were not a high priority for Cambodians in the time between the departure of the Americans in April 1975 and the invasion by Vietnamese troops that toppled the Khmer Rouge government less than four years later. The American bombing and subsequent invasion of Cambodia that began in 1969 were indifferent to the existence of the Cambodian peasants whose lives were disrupted or ended. For the Americans, body counts of the non-existent were likewise not a priority.

6

guns, repressed homosexual leanings hidden beneath their patriotic militarism. They were thumping a few Commie Pinko Radicals, that's all. Or maybe it was all a mistake, a stupid misunderstanding. A crowd, given the right camera perspective and angle, can be mistaken for a mob, and in the right circumstance, anyone with a little military training can become a killer—that's what they're trained to be, after all.

There are reasons why so few can remember what happened. Since 1970 everyone has seen hundreds—no, thousands—of people die. Most days you can see death on the evening news, occasionally quite graphically. Some of the death scenes show the corpses of those who have starved, or are about to starve to death. Every once in a while there will actually be some falling bodies, or film of people who lie twisted and broken and dead in the rubble and wreckage of some far-off terrorist bombing or military skirmish. You see the corpses, but the television news never seems to be quite clear about who or what is responsible for creating those corpses. Then the prime time programs come on, and you can see more deaths—usually highly dramatic, but fictional ones. You know they're just actors pretending to get killed. And the reason why they're dead is explained by the plot of the program, sort of.

On an average day, violence and killing are going to be the fundamental content of television. Or if you think that overstates it a little, I can put it another way. Violence is the content that solves most of the problems that do get solved, whether you

---

What happened in Cambodia between 1969, when the Americans began to bomb the country in an attempt to capture or kill those in the headquarters of the National Liberation Front and the Provisional Revolutionary Government, and to disrupt North Vietnamese supply lines along the Ho Chi Minh Trail, and 1979 when the Vietnamese invaded, is beyond the grasp of statistics. You will understand why if you try to imagine a war in your own country or city or neighbourhood which kills one out of three. A third of your family strangled by a neighbour made psychotic by having been given the power of life and death over everyone he knows, or shot down in the street by a group of adolescents who have replaced the police. Most of your neighbours similarly executed for "criminal tendencies" that

are watching the evening news or prime time dramatic programming. And in the welter of actual or stunt/illusion death and violence even those of us who care about far-off events like Kent State are unable to keep track of the exact details. The students were protesting something, and some of them were killed for it.

So now, sixteen years later, also a sunny morning in May, after the uncounted, unaccountable and largely untelevised deaths of several million more human beings, I try to imagine the last hours of those four students who died at Kent State, to try to learn what I can from them about the deaths that have followed.

The Kent State students were ordinary people. What I mean is that, for example, they probably ate breakfast before coming to the demonstration. Okay, I ask myself, what did they have? Did they have cold cereal and milk, or was it toast, bacon and eggs? Coffee, tea or milk? Perhaps, at the moment the firing began, one of the victims was wondering about lunch. Hamburgers? A milkshake? Was another student worried about a bad grade recently received for a carelessly written English paper?

I discover myself cringing at such speculations. They are brutal and invasive, because they reveal the structure of the Kent State victims' innocence. It is one thing to be in a war zone, a voluntary belligerent, but the Kent State students aren't in a war zone, and they aren't really belligerents. They're similar, in a sense, to the Cambodian peasants who looked up into the

---

are the primary political and social virtues of Western Civilization: religious and political tolerance, loyalty to family and friends, liberality in the face of work-related errors, even simple curiosity. Those who could not hide these "criminal tendencies" have been exterminated. And if you are alive, what is it that you have had to do that has enabled you to survive?

When the National Geographic Society gets around to something it should be possible to take it on faith that the subject is approaching common knowledge. Twenty years ago that might have been true. Most North Americans with an interest in what rose to the undulating surface of public consciousness probably did read the magazine every month. 'Isn't that interesting,' they could say to one another. They

suddenly clamouring skies and discovered that American B-52 bombers were dropping bombs on them. Their "crimes" are the same. Both appeared to be threatening violence to American imperial consciousness. It is hard for an American bomber pilot looking down through his bombsight to see that there is a difference between Cambodian peasants and the Viet Cong soldiers he is trying to kill. A poorly trained and nervous National Guardsman likewise might have trouble seeing the difference between what he suspects are dangerous Commie Pinko Radicals and these nice American students who are thinking about what they'll have for lunch after the demonstration, or if they might want to date the person they've just handed an anti-war placard to. You don't see what people are thinking when you're staring at them down a bombsight or the barrel of a rifle.

The television cameras intrude right here. The television cameras are supposed to establish the facts about our world, to tell us who is who and what is what. So what's wrong with these cameras? Isn't this the era of total information? Or is the mission of television different than announced?

•

Someone once wrote that the only thing that all human beings respond to alike is slapstick. In 50 A.D. for instance, a light-hearted Roman centurion is said to have lifted his tunic and farted loudly into the Jerusalem Passover crowd. Certain zealous

---

might have discussed the details of whatever quaint and picturesque nation was being featured, nodding with a small degree of official and mutual sagacity before they passed on to the next topic of conversation.

But this is the 1980s. That same demographic sector has lost interest in public consciousness and has given up on conversation. People watch television instead, dispensing with the need for either of those. All that is required for social life now is to pass the cans of Pepsi or Coke seen in competing ads, and to repeat something heard or read or seen on television in the last twenty-four hours. In the face of incoming information, citizens take on whatever expression of concern, sagacity or fashionable amusement is appropriate. Sure, there might be a small disquisition over which cola is the better product, or which

celebrants in the crowd took exception to this show of disrespect for their institutions and rituals, and attacked the centurion. A riot ensued, and according to Josephus, who wrote a history of the period and location, by the time Roman troops regained control of the situation, 30,000 people were dead.

Sober-minded interpreters have since removed a zero from Josephus' estimate, thus restoring 27,000 persons to life. It's a strange variety of arithmetic. 30,000 people being killed in a riot over a matter of etiquette is funny in an uncomfortable sort of way. Removing the extremity of the numbers turns the event into something less—just another riot, and history is full of them. And in case you were wondering, it isn't known if the centurion survived his attempt at cultural witticism. Josephus, a Jew who wrote his history in Rome under the supervision of the Emperor, wasn't inclined to indulge in human interest items. And anyway, he may not have thought the centurion was very witty.

How about another one? This one occurred in sixth-century Roman Constantinople. While the city was under siege by a horde of Bulgarians, an argument broke out in the Hippodrome between the two chief political factions, the Blues and the Greens. The argument was not over the best method to defend the city, as might have been expected in the circumstances, but over the nature of Christ. The Blues believed that Christ had a single nature—that he was wholly divine—citing as evidence the fact that his body had not suffered corruption within the

---

ad campaign is the more convincing. Citizens may even wonder if they are aligned with the correct consumer faction, certain only that the shareholders on both sides are going to be winners.

For North Americans living in the 1980s, memory is not yet a crime, and imagination, particularly if it has some entrepreneurial panache, is sometimes rewarded. But within a culture that is attempting to make individual memory and imagination superfluous, both are becoming political acts. God help us.

This isn't a God-help-us story. Invoking a divinity isn't going to work. If there are omniscient beings in the universe, they aren't guiding us. They might be scientists, and this might be an experiment. If it is, it is clearly going to be left alone to run its course.

sepulchre. The Greens believed that Christ's nature was dual—
that he was the son of God, and therefore divine, and the son
of Mary, and therefore human. The argument got out of hand,
and by the time the fighting had ceased, half the city had been
burned, and close to 40,000 people were dead.

These non-strategic anecdotes have survived because they
contain a powerful, if slightly sickening element of slapstick.
Each tells us something about the nature of the times. First-
century Jerusalem apparently didn't have much of a sense of
humour, and sixth-century Constantinople didn't have much
of an instinct for self-preservation. The anecdotes may also have
a warning to deliver to those who insist on the pragmatic nature
of political reality. But the point I get from them is that crowd
control obviously hadn't been honed to the fine science it is
today.

•

With these two incidents in mind, let's go forward to the semi-
present of Kent State to ask a few questions. For me, the
questions that arise from all three events have to do with staging,
and with crowd control. I seem to recall that the television
cameramen who filmed the events at Kent State had initially
set up their cameras midway between the demonstrators and
the National Guardsmen, almost as if they were about to film
a battle between approaching armies. Such scenes were common

Even that's too easy. This isn't a story about being alone or one
about being left alone to fend for ourselves. This is a story about
memory and imagination, and about the reorganizations of human
intelligence that are about to leave us all in a new—or a very ancient—
kind of darkness. It is a story about what Cambodia means, and about
why Cambodia is not an isolated historical aberration suitable for sentimental speculation and pictorial depiction. Cambodia is as near as
your television set.

This is a century in which the lives of at least 100 million of us have
ended prematurely: by war, civil violence, or by the disease and famine
that usually accompany war or civil disruption. All 100 million deaths
were avoidable, given the wealth and technological capability of human

then—long-haired demonstrators meeting with armed soldiers and placing flowers into the barrels of the rifles under the watchful lens of the television cameras.

But at Kent State there is no such peaceful congress at the midpoint of the battlefield. When the National Guardsmen start firing at the students, there is confusion. The cameras swing first to the source of the shots, then to the recipients. A student, hit by a bullet, falls, and a second student rushes to his aid, shielding his comrade from further violence with his own body. Most of the rest of the crowd scatters.

The cameras swing back to the Guardsmen. They also are in disarray. Backs are turned, there are accusatory gestures.

An interval—in real time, but not in the always sequential reality of television. The wounded are being attended to. The dead or dying students are shielded from the camera lenses, bodies are covered by coats. A female student screams at a cameraman, tries to put her hands in front of the prying lens.

Repeat this sequence several million times.

•

Now the ideological question: what is in control? It is now twenty-four hours after the event. The film has been edited into a more coherent package. The first thing to note is that the "action" sequence has been rearranged and cut back. The guardsmen are seen firing their rifles, mostly into the air. A

---

civilization. They weren't avoided.

The dominant political and social facts of our century are contradictory. Radically so. We have experienced unprecedented levels of social control, both benevolent and/or authoritarian. But we have also seen unprecedented levels of social and political violence. Governments, which are supposed to protect us from violence, have been intervening in social and economic activities more and more in order to make the world safe. More and more as the century has progressed. In fact, the continuous growth of authority and bureaucracy is a universal phenomenon of modern political life. But bureaucratic authority has a most unexpected twin: genocide.

•

very quick and blurry clip depicts one of the students falling. An even briefer clip shows a body being placed in an ambulance. The confusion of the National Guardsmen that was so evident in the initial film has been edited out, along with the irate female student who screamed at the cameraman. A National Guard spokesman with brass buttons and medals states with great gravity that an investigation is underway.

The television reporter, with the empty green lawns and genteel buildings of Kent State University as his backdrop, reports a rumour currently circulating that the first shots came from the direction of the demonstrating students, and that the guardsmen were responding to that. Police are said to be investigating the possibility of a sniper located in the nearby buildings. The camera duly pans to an open second floor window. The final images return us to the scene of the event. It is empty of National Guardsmen and students, and of the realities of death and slapstick. Order has been imposed.

But four students are dead, their families and friends are grieving, and American combat troops and equipment are moving forward through the jungles of Cambodia, trying to find Viet Cong who are going to be somewhere else when the bombs drop or the troops arrive.

There's no slapstick in any of this, right? These are all facts, a matter of historical documentation. Yet the message television delivers doesn't contain those facts. Instead, it tells us that the authorities are on top of the situation, and that everything being

---

I suppose this is also a story about me, which is to say, about private authority. In specific terms, that will be a story about what it means to be intellectually and artistically adrift in North America in the 1980s, a hostile in the Global Village, and about what must be remembered by private authors in the years after history has ceased, for the first time in three hundred years, to provide form to public reality.

I don't trust any authority, and that is a problem. Not a unique problem for an author these days. I see bureaucracy and genocide infecting every human act, the one destroying productivity and memory, the other undermining the ability to imagine a future. Yet to be an author involves exerting authority over one's subject matter. How do

done is fine and orderly and rational. It doesn't tell us *what* is in control. That question has been atomized by implied conspiracies, allegations, rumours, technically opaque editing. Don't ask.

I'm not quite convinced. The atomized particles regroup in my mind, and create more questions. Where does television stand on the question of crowd control? Which crowd is being controlled? Are all of us walking with the students at Kent State, or standing armed with the National Guardsmen? Or are we all looking through the camera lens? Which part of this tableau are you in? Where will you be when the firing starts? Is violence inevitable? Where are we all now, sixteen years later, when the slapstick of ordinary life is almost entirely invisible? Can we allow our utopian dreams of a just world to be an uncomfortable memory we avoid as we try to hang onto our personal possessions in a slowly shrinking economy and quickly diminishing public reality? Is our desire to be told the truth going to become a side-screen evanescence as we click off the television set and go about the strange lives we are left with?

I write without falling into the enemy camp?

The surface of public consciousness in the 1980s has been made astonishingly difficult to penetrate because of the massive array of covertly-interpreted data and propaganda thrown into the path of the contemporary investigator. The ugly truths of our time are neither dark nor silent. They have been rendered opaque by full-frequency light that admits neither definition nor shadows, and they are protected from the voices of the suffering and the disaffected by an accompanying wall of white noise.

At first, Cambodia appears to be an exception to the currents of modern political history. The Khmer Rouge administrative massacres were perpetrated by Asian Marxists on other Asians; the apparatus

A Small Committee

Say, for the fun of it, we're in a small room, you and I. On one wall is a two-way mirror that looks out into a larger room. It is a meeting room, furnished with a rectangular oak veneer table and padded black vinyl chairs. A dozen people are sitting around the table. I've invited you here because I have a story about those twelve people which I want to get you interested in. Maybe you're an executive from a large television network, and I'm a writer trying to sell you an idea for a television series. Here's the story:

Most of the people in the committee room have been meeting once a week for a decade. They're sitting around the table in a visibly limited variety of stereotyped postures, most of which they've learned from self-help manuals. The postures are familiar—they're meant to create illusions of positive social characteristics: confidence, aggressiveness, reflectiveness. These postures are important to the individuals here. If they weren't, the postures wouldn't be so rigid. But they're also a key to the makeup of the committee. Over the ten years, not one member

---

and victims alike are foreign. The killings were halted by another nation of Asian Marxists—the first time a Marxist government has deposed another Marxist government. None of it is our responsibility, right? Certainly the polite argot of *National Geographic* magazine invites us to think of Cambodia as a remote darkness, an inexplicable horror.

I can't quite accept that. Nothing is inexplicable. Either I don't have adequate information, or I am ignoring information. Admittedly, Cambodia is dark and silent, unlike my world, where all is impenetrable light and white noise. I will therefore enter and explore the apparent darkness of Cambodia, not to experience the inexplicable horror, but to uncover and unlock the subterranean entrances to my

has changed an opinion or belief. Not one has altered the nexus of isolated facts, opinions and self-postures out of which each constructs their personal reality. There is considerable precision in what these people do here.

You frown. How do I know what goes on in these people's minds? It's clear they aren't fictional. Typical, in a boring sort of way, but not the kind of typicality television thrives on. Well, I could offer you personal testimony. I could say, *I was there*. But to be honest, I don't believe that means much. Instead, I offer a different kind of testimony: *these people are worth your time*. Indulge me a little.

This committee you're looking at is about what it appears to be. It is a fairly typical contemporary political institution: a government-funded policy coordinating committee with terms of reference that demand that it achieve a broad-based consensus. That's the official description. In the argot of the Liberal Left it is designed to co-opt citizen energies, and in the language of the Right it is a ploy to keep bureaucrats busy wasting tax dollars and holding up development.

The members, however, have long since ceased to attach sensory, historical, and technical data to any collective terms of reference. They ascribe all actions to psychological motivations and they attach data to their own opinions. Without recognizing it, they've all decided that there are no objective facts left in the debate, and that information (and history along with it) is relevant only insofar as it supports their opinions.

---

own world.

2

On or about the 29th of May, 1890, Joseph Conrad, a passenger on the French steamer *La Ville de Maceio* out of Bordeaux bound for Matadi in what is now Zaire, observed a French warship shelling, for no apparent reason, a stretch of the African coastline. For Conrad, this curious tableau, noted almost casually in his journal, was the first small breaker signalling what was to become a tidal wave. The events that engulfed Conrad in the next several months would turn him from a career as a mariner and an adventurer to one as a seden-

Some of them find this frustrating, but since important matters are at stake, they've learned to live with the frustration. This is tactical struggle, they say, and the rewards will go to those who win, not to those who argue fairly or uphold the antiquated laws of discourse. Each member knows what will serve their interests, and therefore what is good, right and situationally correct. Together, these knowledges make up 'the reality of the situation'. And the further from the 'reality of the situation' a person's opinions stray the more "unreal" that person will be to the other committee members. By definition, this is a room full of monsters and freaks.

Not a very auspicious beginning, is it? So far, no movement, no spectacular acts, no stunts, no hint of surrealism or science fiction. You note only that my face is pressed to the mirror, that I am fascinated by this scene, these people. You lean your hand against the mirror, and I have to catch your hand to keep you from revealing our presence by tapping impatiently against the mirror's surface.

A female committee member stands up to address the committee. By her own evaluation she is a 'nice' person. She is that and more; a pleasant looking woman, confident in her manners and expensively if casually dressed, the wife of a wealthy and successful lawyer. The committee has been the means by which she has gained a large degree of that evident self-confidence—so much so that some of the more cynical members of the committee, half-jokingly, say that she is the

---

tary writer who rarely strayed beyond the confines of his own study. As a writer he was to provide the world with its first and perhaps most profound glimpses into the contrary nature of reality in the twentieth century: that an almost identical barbarity grows out of an overabundance of technological wealth as comes from its relative absence.

At the time he saw the warship shelling the jungle, Conrad thought of himself as a romantic adventurer about to fulfill a childhood dream of exploring a barely known part of Africa. He had no idea of what he was about to find in the Congo, and he could have had no more than an inkling that he was to become a writer. He'd known about what writers were from his childhood, and he knew what happened

committee's biggest success, its one substantial product. Today, she will speak on the question of natural rights, which to her are the same as property rights.

But before she speaks, let me outline the ostensible subject matter the committee has been debating. It is the building of an airport runway. The arm of the government set up to service the air industry wants to build a new runway for the growth in air traffic it has projected. That the growth predicted ten years ago has not materialized does not deter this government department in the least. The department's statisticians continue to project vast and patently unreasonable levels of growth, readjusting their 'targets' each year in accordance with the development-oriented logic of their mandate rather than from any data on actual increases in passengers and planes or from any coherent view of what the future may involve.

The chief opponent of these government airport developers is a community group: Association Against Airtransport. The airport developers and their allies have another name for the group: Assholes Assaulting Aircraft.

Between those two polarities is a spectrum of middle class personalities, institutions, and the government departments created to service their tastes: environmental agencies; a metropolitan government planning bureau made up of city governments affected by the airport; private environmental lobbies; and private air industry associations—flying clubs and representatives of the major airlines. Presiding over the

---

to them in an uncaring mercantile world. His father had been a romantic poet and playwright in his native Poland, and as a child, Conrad had watched as his father was destroyed by romantic illusions about literature and political reality. In a sense, it is ironic that Conrad was headed for what he believed was a romantic job as the captain of a Congo river steamer. He hadn't lost his taste for romance. He must have believed that the fate of adventurers is one thing and the fate of poets is another.

Conrad's Congo job was not a romantic adventure. He witnessed a sequence of horrors that came close to destroying his sanity. It did take his health and his zest for adventure. The mercantile world exposed its dark, redolent underbelly to him in that isolated outpost,

committee—providing a chairman and funding the deliberations—is a government agency which has the singular mandate of 'promoting and enhancing democratic participation'.

"The building of this runway is an infringement on the rights of people to reasonable privacy," says the woman, drawing herself into a rhetorical pose of righteousness. "And I want my children to be able to grow up..."

"In complete privacy," concludes one of the air industry officials, with a snigger to his superior, who sits next to him, shuffling through a stack of technical reports.

The woman peers at the two men, raises her eyebrows slightly, and goes on with her speech, undeterred by their predictable solecisms. She talks about her children, not in a sentimental or anecdotal way, but with moral certitude and the right reason it generates. She tells the committee of her profound belief in the perfect innocence of children, arguing that the existence of such innocence presupposes natural rights. It is one thing, as far as she is concerned, to impose something evil and wasteful on adults, and quite another to impose it on innocent children.

"The future belongs to my children," she says, looking up triumphantly. "I'm here today as I've been here from the beginning, because I want the world they live in to be a free and decent one."

Everyone on the committee solemnly nods assent to this.

"If the kind of public funds the government wants to spend on building unnecessary runways and gold-plated terminal

---

and it showed him authority's teeth, hungry for corpses. Yet somehow, it did not take his taste for romance. Instead, it honed it into a weapon that allowed him to pierce that underbelly, and to reveal some of its darkest contents. Quite probably he came to understand the teeth, and what it was that kept them sharp. But by then he was a prudent man, an immigrant, and it was not very far into the twentieth century. He kept his counsel.

Conrad eventually published two fictional accounts of his voyage into the heart of the Congo, the now-famous *Heart of Darkness*, and the more obscure *An Outpost of Progress*. Both are tales about how God doesn't help anyone.

■

buildings are so readily available," she continues, extending the logic of her previous statement in a way that surprises no one on the committee, "I suggest that they be reallocated to services that more people can use on a daily basis, like better public transit and improved community facilities and things like that."

The same official who earlier made the sniggering remark to his superior, and who had, during the speech, given the appearance that he was attempting to stare a hole in the back of his knuckles, suddenly straightens in his chair and interrupts.

"How did you get to the meeting today, Mrs. Turnbull?" he asks mildly. "Did you take a bus?"

Alisha Turnbull hasn't used public transit in her adult life, and her questioner knows it. She is flustered for a few seconds, her jaw flapping open as she looks around for support.

"I couldn't take the bus because I had to drop my children off at the community centre for their ballet lessons," she replies after a moment, regaining her composure and moving to the attack. "And I was late. Not everybody can just drop what they're doing and jump on a bus to a meeting, you know. Some people have other responsibilities. Some of the members of this committee come here without being paid, and it's a great deal of trouble to be here on time."

Roughly half of the committee signal their agreement. The other half squirm with fake umbrage or a more real impatience.

The chairman, an even-tempered man in his early forties who

Like almost all of Conrad's work, *Heart of Darkness*, considered solely as a work of art, is flawed. This may account, in part, for its popularity among college professors, who have used it for decades to illustrate to students the academic virtues and ideas the professors happen to espouse, most of which have nothing to do with the subject matter of the story or with Conrad's own erratic but frequently brilliant insights into his own linguistic and intellectual predilections.

I was first forced to deal with the story as part of the requirements for a freshman university literature course. My initial response was to refuse to read the book. I cynically did my assignments and wrote the exam solely on the information provided by the professor. This man, basing his teaching on the crib printed as a preface to the

thinks of himself as a professional 'chairperson', breaks up the skirmish.

"Can we perhaps get on with the proceedings?" he asks in a professionally conciliatory tone that deliberately reveals a slight weariness. "We have a number of pressing items on our agenda."

•

And we have a number of pressing items on *our* agenda, you and I. The uninteresting vignette of modern bureaucratic life I have recorded for you is a significant one. It is significant precisely because it is *dull*. And its dullness doesn't derive from the subject matter. The question of what the proper distribution of wealth should be isn't a dull subject. If you can find a more important one, I'd like to hear about it. About 500 million dollars are involved in this particular subset of the question. That's a pretty interesting sum.

What makes the discussion of it dull is that no member of the committee sees the need to risk the carefully nurtured and protected illusions and opinions by which they secure their self-credibility in order to bring the discussion to some sort of resolution. They expect the argument to be resolved elsewhere, at a higher level.

Nor is any member of the committee prepared to interrupt the dullness of the proceedings by some extraordinary dramatic

---

Official College Text, informed me that the story was about The Darkness—the secret one that resides in the recesses of every human mind.

I hated Joseph Conrad and his story. Even more, I hated the idea, as offered up by my professor, that there was darkness at the core of the human psyche. I was twenty-two at the time, self-educated in the erratic manner of one who migrates from an isolated outpost of the Imperium and is filled with an ambition to understand all of its Imperial workings. Conrad—or the Conrad presented to me by my genteel professor—seemed to propose that my ambition was preposterous and naive.

In those days, I had a simpler notion of what darkness was. Darkness

action, such as pulling a small but lethal pistol from a purse or briefcase and spraying the room with bullets—something that more than one of them would do if they thought they could get their hands on the $500 million and make a break for it. That they do not, I at least am prepared to be glad.

But no one on this committee is even willing to pinch their neighbour to see, as the saying goes, if they are real. And that is a problem that both you and I share, and so does everyone else. I'm willing to argue that this makes them at least as dangerous as a dozen terrorists bent on blowing up an airport terminal.

"So," you ask, suppressing a yawn, "who are these people?"

Well, they are modern and typical and quite certainly decent people, as you can see. The social panorama they present isn't quite the last supper as recorded by Leonardo da Vinci, but they are a modern equivalent, in line with the definition that Sartre has given to the modern image of humanity: *a small committee surrounded by adoring animals.*

In fact, if you'll indulge a digression for a moment, the committee is what used to be called the Elect, although nobody has elected these people to sit on the committee. Some of them have been ordered to be here by their superiors. Most of the rest have got themselves appointed to the committee because they believe they represent morally and tactically superior interests, and are situationally accountable to no single person or authority. They are inspired by that liberty to account for

---

was error. Errors could be corrected. But the kind of darkness my college instructor was talking about when he taught me Conrad was brand new. It was psychological, absolute, and without the possibility of alteration. I'd already convinced myself that psychology was itself a variety of evil, that it sought not so much to illuminate the darkened places of the mind as it did to glorify them or to invent ways to manipulate them.

I'd read Rousseau, and I'd chosen to believe, with Rousseau, that human life was an involvement with light. I saw myself as a modernized version of Rousseau's noble savage, and probably I wasn't far off. I'd come from my outpost seeking the light of civilization, ready to participate in its brilliant labours. I was not prepared to entertain

the well-being of all who fall within their definition of acceptable humanity. Some of these same people, of course, are entirely sincere in their desire to serve the public interest as they see it.

After ten years, how they got here and why they came doesn't explain why they've stayed. Now they're here by a single common agreement; the necessary existence of the committee.

You're staring at the ceiling now. No matter. Let me pursue this idea of the Elect. After all, it's been around as long as Judaeo-Christian civilization has, and it is very close to our core values.

To be a member of the Elect is to be among the Chosen. Judaism invented the idea of the Elect around three thousand years ago as a response to the tribal pluralism of a primitive world. It was a means of protecting their not-very-powerful tribe against political aggression and cultural decay. Unlike most of their neighbours, the Jews had one rather authoritarian god, Yahweh, who chose their twelve tribes as the subject of his irritable and abstract attentions. The idea of the Elect has worked remarkably well. The Jews have stuck together as no other embattled culture has been able to.

As the world began to fill up with human beings, Judaism's high degree of civil organization attracted converts, and the concept of the Elect changed. The Judaic Elect became, in practice, the priestly class. When Apostolic Christianity emerged —possibly because of this subtle redefinition—it reduced the concept of the Elect from that of twelve pure tribes to twelve

---

the notion that there was an unalterable darkness at the core of all human consciousness. Had I believed that, I would have stayed where I'd grown up and fulfilled my natural destiny. My father was a moderately prosperous merchant, and it was intended that I would be the true son of my father and follow in his footsteps, manufacturing and delivering marginally necessary consumer products to the inhabitants of our rapidly growing outpost.

The civilization I'd come to join was one that I believed would be governed by knowledge and energized by education. I believed that my fellow men and women were creatures of light, and (then as now) I thought that we were meant for better things than we seemed to be getting. Most strongly of all, I believed that the human mind should

pure men, thus creating an astonishingly efficient administrative system that easily wiped out most of the wilder elements of the new religion and kept the rest under control for 1500 years. Then Martin Luther and John Calvin came along and changed the idea of the Elect once again.

Admittedly, at various times during history, being Chosen hasn't been all that much fun, particularly if one was from the Judaeo part of the formula. But in the last five hundred years or so, especially if you happen to be of Anglo-Saxon or Teutonic Protestant descent, you have had a pretty good chance of becoming part of an Elect that has been drowning in self-inflicted spiritual and economic gravy. As the idea of God has drifted away from its original jealously stern and authoritarian image and closer to that of a Rotary Club president, the Elect have had to create and then act upon increasingly arbitrary and individualistic values and patterns of action. And meanwhile, we've arrived back at the historical situation where the idea started: an incoherent pluralist world. But it isn't tribal anymore. It's simply every self-chosen man for himself.

Originally, to be part of the Elect simply meant that you were part of the tribe and accountable to it. The Protestant canon has changed that. The Elect are chosen—no doubt to illustrate the inscrutable superiority of divine logic—without regard to origin, suitability or merit. The implication is that God simply gets the hots for some people.

On the other end of this self-serving spectrum of divine favour,

---

not be tampered with or manipulated for ulterior purposes. I recognized nothing of myself in my instructor's depiction of Conrad, nor in his depiction of Conrad's Manichean portrait of humanity. There was no darkness in me, and I had no interest in the opportunities that darkness seemed to enable.

I didn't like my instructor much better than I liked Conrad. My instructor was implying that a truly educated person is apolitical, and that he or she quietly attends the dark mysteries of the mind, uninterested in the vulgar and visible struggles of the material world. I quickly figured out that apoliticality was a self-serving and self-deluding political position, one that was invariably reactionary. But it was not my place then to argue openly with my instructor for the

there is a group who are chosen for God's target practice. No matter what these people do, they are made to suffer torment and damnation. In the original Judaic usage, these are the Reprobates—Canaanites, and other Semitic tribes who should have accepted the authority of Jehovah but didn't. In the Apostolic Christian interpretation, this group has consisted of slaves, peasants, and until a few years ago, the working class and/or the lumpen proletariat. But now, as in Judaic times, with the world crowded with non-believers, there is another group between the Elect and the Reprobates. They are called, depending on your orientation, Gentiles, the Public, the People, the Silent Majority, the Masses, the Great Unwashed, the Mob, the Demographic Midrange—an almost endless list of terms, each of which explains the particular orientation in the perspective of the person using the term, and not much else.

You're waving your hands in my face as if you've decided that I've gone into some sort of trance. You're thinking that nobody is going to watch this. It's just too damned slow—a bunch of boring bureaucrats arguing with equally boring citizens. That, and all this nonsense about the twelve tribes of Israel and biblical theory just doesn't possess scriptable possibilities. The Ten Commandments has been done to death, and religion is a commercial no-no for all but the evangelists. No commercial potential. You try to ease past me, attempting to make a break for it.

Not so fast. I push you back and fix an Ancient Mariner gaze

---

primacy of an improvable and material reality. A pragmatist, I said nothing. The instructor had his textbook, his university tenure, an expensive house in the suburbs. And he had my grades in his hands.

I was thirty before I finally came to read Conrad, and even then it was the result of a fortunate accident. I blundered onto a little book written by Mark Twain in 1905 entitled *King Leopold's Soliloquy*. The subject was the Belgian Congo, and within a few pages I recognized that I'd seriously misjudged Joseph Conrad. The heart of darkness he'd written about had a physical location and was a complex of material events and consequences. It was secret, but it wasn't psychological.

From Twain's pamphlet I learned that the Congo river basin had

on you. If you think, for one second, that the idea of the Elect no longer applies, please think again. There is not a single political, economic, social or interpersonal structure in the industrialized world that does not have its Elect, its Reprobates, and that third and ill-defined class that now funds and consumes most of the products of the structure.

And another thing. I'm no radical. I'm not saying the Elect are evil. Certainly not on this committee. They're all pursuing righteous causes. Ask them. If you prod anyone in public life they'll admit to being in hot pursuit of righteousness. And many will tell you they possess it. The committee in our story, for instance, both possesses it and pursues it on behalf of what they call 'The Public'.

And remember, our committee is at a deadlock, and has been from its beginning. It has defined the boundaries of its concerns. It assumes that it is the absolute perimeter of contemporary reality and has created a series of armed fortresses of camouflaged self-interest and self-concern to guard them. Nothing gets in. And nothing gets out. You and I can leave our mirrored room, but it will make no difference. We will still be subject, one way or another, to the non-action of the committee or that of a hundred thousand like it.

Stop rolling your eyeballs. This is as real a modern drama as you'll ever see. For instance, do you know what happens from here? I don't. But I do know that since the committee is deadlocked, and since it can imagine no other condition than

---

been the site of perhaps the most extensive series of massacres in human history. In 1890, by International Treaty, the Belgian Congo was constituted as the "Congo Free State", under the personal control and supervision of Leopold II, the King of Belgium. In the next two decades, Leopold gave new and brutal definition to the saying *L'état, c'est moi*. The Congo became the largest private plantation in history. The chief commodity produced by the plantation was rubber. The profits from it went more or less directly into the bank accounts of the Belgian monarch.

The Congo of the 1890s was densely populated but culturally diffuse and technologically extremely primitive. There was a plethora of tribal groups, all living in small territorially organized enclaves, all hostile

to be deadlocked, and since the deadlock is its accurate and ultimate statement on the human condition, anything I write from here on will involve violating both the subject and the subject's subject matter: the deadlocked committee and their concept of themselves as the Elect. Even my brief description of Alisha Turnbull sent the story careening off course. You— or perhaps it was only I—got interested in her. No, I'm sure I caught a glimmer of curiosity in your eyes. Were you trying to imagine her on-screen? What colour is her hair? How many children does she have? Do we see the children, perhaps as a subplot item? How much money did her husband lose in the recent real estate debacle?

As the writer of this tale, I have a problem with that kind of interest, because it isn't what the story is about. I also have an even larger problem to solve.

Here it is. If I stick to the story on the terms by which the committee approaches both itself and the world outside the committee room, I don't have much of a story. It lacks excitement, there's no plot and none of the other conventional attributes of narrative. The members just sit there, bored and probably unhappy with the committee and with life itself. But at the same time, they are self-satisfied; they can imagine no other kind of action, no other kind of world. The logical thing for me to do is to stop writing; and for you, to stop listening to me and walk out mumbling irritably about time-wasting jerks. There's much easier material for television, and we both know it.

---

and isolated from one another, and all operating close to the margin of subsistence.

The rubber was collected in the following manner. The administration of the Free State, backed by an armed constabulary (conscripted largely from one of the more aggressive tribal groups), would appear in a village to set and collect taxes and to spread, as they put it, the progressive and uplifting ethic of hard work. The village being subjected to this enlightened form of "taxation" was ordered, during the taxation period, to produce a quota of raw rubber and to support the supervisory apparatus of the Free State.

These quotas could not be met without curtailing or abandoning the agricultural and food-gathering practices that enabled the villagers

But before you give up on me and my silly difficulties, think of the difficulties the committee faces: they're real people, and they have to live with this dead-ended reality and its absence of nourishing narrative. And they're not unique. They're close enough to home to make me nervous, and the chances are that they're pretty similar to you. You may, in your public life, sit on a committee like theirs.

The greater part of the middle classes are deadlocked in this committee or others like it, trying to be righteous for other people. And as a result, the reactionary classes to their political right and left are running amok, taking over control of the world, creating a shambles of the orderly progression toward universal social justice which is the cherished and sustaining goal of a democracy. So maybe you should sit still for a few more paragraphs.

Let's return to the problems I have as a writer. Art imitates Life, right? And Life is dynamic, right? But what if Life's dynamic has come to resemble that of the committee, and Art—which naturally gravitates toward conventional powers and techniques in order to identify the narrative that will catch the largest possible audience—what if Art is imitating the committee?

Most of the fiction written today is doing just that. How else can Danielle Steel, Robert Ludlum, or Stephen King be explained? They have planted themselves and their techniques at the centre of the place in the human psyche which seeks to

---

to subsist. What little food was produced went first to the colonial supervisory apparatus—the constabulary. Within weeks a rapid breakdown of tribal structure and morale occurred. Within months, the result was widespread malnutrition and/or starvation. The weak or ill, unable to secure the required rubber quotas, were killed or chased into the jungle to die. The corpses of the dead villagers were piled in the village as disciplinary encouragement for those that continued to survive. When the entire village had been exterminated, the apparatus simply packed up and moved on to the next terrified village, and the process was repeated.

I found Twain's pamphlet disturbing and exciting, but I also found it hard to digest. There was a gap in it, and I couldn't figure out what

understand itself, its environment, and the uniquely human craving for narrative. And everything these writers do is a denial of the possibility of such understanding. Surrealists, all of them.

Surrealists? That's right. Surrealism is a response—probably one that operates at a molecular level—to incomprehensible complexity. Its first modern appearance, and its most honest one, was after the First World War, which showed us the dark side of all the marvellous technological advances of the preceding decades. But that war—specifically trench warfare—was incomprehensible to the men who experienced it. Those who survived were haunted by its imagery into producing a rational theory of irrationality, one that hallucinated itself into every known way of perceiving human actions and interactions. Sure, the movement later on became the artistic style to which it has now descended. But at one time it was a desperate and beautiful invention.

Surrealism has been tamed. Even made popular, to the point where Stephen King can use its techniques. Lately it has become respectable and middle class. A committee formed to discuss the spending of half a billion dollars on an airport that will enable travellers coming home from vacations in Hawaii or Mexico or China to avoid the unpleasant experience of carrying their suitcases a hundred yards in the rain, while half the people in the world are suffering from malnutrition, is surrealism.

•

---

it was. I began to read Conrad, but I also researched the question further. It was something I found in Hannah Arendt, months later, that showed me what the gap was.

It was a single sentence. I found it as a tag end to a complex discussion of totalitarian administrative brutality. She was illustrating different instances of such brutality, and the Congo was among her examples. Between 1890 and 1910, to use her indifferent enumeration, between 15 and 40 million Africans died in the Congo, either by murder or starvation.

I reread the sentence several times, trying to understand what it was about it that so disturbed me. At first I couldn't see it. 40 million human deaths was an astonishing figure, but it was one I'd already

I know. Now I've completely lost track of my original subject. A few paragraphs back I was discussing the Elect, and now I've turned them into a bunch of surrealists in three-piece suits. What next? you ask. Flying Saucers? Armageddon?

No. This is enough: *a small committee surrounded by adoring animals*. How peaceful it is, how much more static and unthreatened by change than, say, *The Last Supper*. Alisha Turnbull, who is played by Mary Tyler Moore, completes her speech, sits down and folds her hands in her lap, awaiting a neutralizing reply from the bureaucrats. Bambi and Thumper watch, munching on the Disneyfied backdrop. Purple cows from your old Sunday school pamphlets crop grass and stare. Lassie and Rin-Tin-Tin sit nearby, their ears pricked forward, alert.

Beyond, in the surrounding golden fields, peasants cut and stook wheat. In the distance, a city with elegant spires and geometric freeways bleeding silent traffic from its heart. An airliner—a Boeing 747—seeks a runway to land on. Now what happens?

Well, just for laughs, how about some Stephen King? Thumper hops over to Alisha Turnbull's chair, attracted by the sheen of her expensive nylons. His lips curl back in a soulless grin, exposing sharp fangs. Without warning Thumper buries his fangs in Alisha's ankle, severing an artery....

Okay, I'll stop. But that's what television and Stephen King have proved the public wants. Or perhaps the peasants drop their sickles, take AK47 rifles from under the piles of wheat

---

got from Twain. Eventually it came to me. It was the construction of the sentence itself, its placement in the argument, and the incredible gap between 15 and 40 million. Arendt, or at least her language and her analytical method, was apparently insensitive to 25 million human lives. Or deaths.

The victims of the Congo massacres wouldn't have been able to conceive of such numbers. For them, their village existed, along with its customs and immediate environs. Perhaps several more villages existed beyond it. The jungle existed, the trails cut through it existed, the river and the starry night sky existed. But the idea of 15 or 40 million dead would have been beyond their grasp.

On the other hand, the sophisticated institutions and individuals

and advance on the committee. Perhaps the 747 crashes. A mushroom cloud blossoms behind the city.

It's either that, or something more dramatic: break up the committee, disband the Elect and its brittle covenant with righteousness. Open our eyes to the world as it is. Let the adoring animals be equal at last.

No matter what you do from here, that's the story we're all in.

---

in the civilized world process and exploit such numbers quite casually. The civilized world is also casually capable of murder on the same scale. But it must do so with a certain sense of unreality, as witnessed by Arendt's incredible statement.

A human death is an event, an extinguishing of consciousness. Because death is an ultimate event to the person who dies and to those who know that person, any intellectual procedure that translates the ultimacy of death into statistics is degrading the value of consciousness, and attacking its reality—committing an act of barbarism.

But, it is impossible for any person, primitive or civilized, to imagine 15 or 40 million individual deaths. An attempt to comprehend death on these kind of sequential enumerative terms will, and should, lead to madness. For these reasons, and for some other reasons that aren't so attractive, the memory of the Congo massacres has been obliterated from Western consciousness and even from the memory of those African tribal cultures that were subjected to it.

Some of us are merely ignorant about the Congo, and some, like Arendt, use more sophisticated means to avoid or ignore the humane meaning of the numbers. I discovered that I could neither remain ignorant nor avoid the numbers—particularly the 25 million human beings immaterialized by Arendt's bland statistification. I found myself, as an artist and as a citizen, being drawn into that gap. Even here, I feel compelled to attempt to make the gap materially comprehensible:

The Belgian Administration of the Congo Free State developed a

The Entrepreneur of God

On a dusty road leading to what is now Damascus, Syria, in the decades just after the death of Jesus Christ nearly two thousand years ago, a man had a vision. That vision changed the world, and it has altered the ways in which human beings have been able to live in the world.

The man wasn't the first to have a vision. Visionary experience was more common then than it is now. But his vision was spectacularly different from the kinds of visions people had in those days, although you and I see and hear visions like his rather frequently. And since the human species is not going to survive much longer if it doesn't find some way to supplant his variety of vision, we had better understand it more clearly.

I'm talking about Saint Saul, Paul of Tarsus, Saul of Tarsus. He is arguably the most important of the Christian Apostles. His philosophical imprint is all over Christianity—he is responsible for authoring more than a third of the New Testament, and probably wrote the most influential of its texts. The depth of his impact on the Christian canon is rarely

---

number of idiosyncratic administrative practices that allow the colossal brutality and injustice of those years to be approached, if not comprehended. Perhaps the most bizarre practice was the procedure developed to account for the distribution and use of rifle cartridges by the constabulary. Rifle cartridges were an expense the colonial administration had to deduct from profits, and therefore became an item to be carefully controlled. The constabulary, in the interest of efficient cartridge husbandry, was made to account for bullets expended not with the spent cartridge hulls, but with severed human right hands.

By itself this reveals that the primary role of the constabulary was not to control unco-operative tribesmen or to encourage production,

disputed seriously. If Peter was the rock on which the Church was built, Paul was the sculptor of that rock. Yet Paul's role has never quite been seen accurately. Perhaps this is a natural consequence of Christianity's diffidence about discussing the source of its success, which it has ascribed either to its mass appeal, or, as all religions do, to an accurate connection with divinity. Paul had little to say on these questions, or at least little that could be described as original. What was original about him was that he provided Christianity with its administrative apparatus, an apparatus that has been the most effective in human history.

•

Paul was an administrative genius and an entrepreneur. A sweet combination, those on the political Right will say. To be sure, the world is currently full of entrepreneurial visionaries. The ground on which Paul walked as he approached his visionary moment is doubly hallowed: by the partisan rhetoric of Christianity and by the Rotary Club. He is an ancient Henry Ford, or Lee Iacocca dressed up in a burnous. But how do those of us who distrust such partisan rhetoric understand this man and his contribution to the control of human beings and their imaginations?

The available scholarship isn't much help. One quickly gets the sense that there is more to Saint Paul than meets the eye

---

but to exterminate human beings. But saying so flatly is like the rest of the possible explanations of bureaucratic logic—abstraction that fails to tell the story. It has to be told in greater detail, as in the following:

Should a bored patrol wander into the jungle to hunt or to indulge in some target practice, the accounting procedure compelled them to enter the nearest village and to collect their quota of human hands, usually from the less economically useful elderly, or from women and children.

•

Shortly after the turn of the century, sufficient international pressure

of either partisan or academic history. For the Christian partisans, Paul is a messenger of God, divinely inspired, and therefore not subject to psychological investigations. His humanity is played down, partly because it is not easily discerned, and partly because the writers are indifferent to it. On the other hand, academic historians, as usual, are too concerned with establishing their phalanxes of dates and imperial facts to be interested in the peculiarities of this figure.

Aside from methodological considerations, they're missing out on a hell of a lot of intellectual fun. Paul is an extraordinarily complicated figure—almost inscrutable by any conventional historiographical method. Presumably no one is reading this for a thousand page concordance of scripture, or for pedantic speculations about his whereabouts on a given day or month or year. So, I feel free to make some speculations on how he came to be on the road to Damascus, and some hopefully amusing and highly relevant calculations of what happened there.

I believe that a series of complicated cultural energies converged in this man. Most of those same currents are present in our own epoch, albeit in somewhat altered form. That being the case, I'm going to do something unorthodox. I'm going to give Paul's visionary conversion a modern witness. This man will be no anonymous secretary or yes-man, but a catalytic figure known almost as well to us as he will be to Paul in my fictional account.

Let's see. Iacocca is busy saving the auto industry and

---

had mounted that it led to the dismantling of the Congo Free State. Some of that pressure was a result of the efforts of humanitarians like Twain, who managed to secure photographs of a few victims that survived hand-severing incidents, and Sir Roger Casement, who wrote a report in 1903 for the British Government that, among other things, documented the hand-severing practice. Conrad had met Casement in Matadi in 1890, and had formed a friendship with him. Casement brought the report to Conrad before he submitted it to the Foreign Office, and tried to enlist his support. There is no record of what Conrad contributed to it, if anything, and Conrad declined the invitation to make a public statement about the report and the events and practices it documented.

wondering if he should run for the U.S. presidency, so he's not available. I can't think of a single academic or clergyman who isn't going to be offended by this, so they're out. The Hudson Institute and the other think-tanks are agoraphobic, and besides, they'd just want to sign him to an exclusive consultant contract. Journalists will just engage in their own peculiar fictive conventions. Ahah! I have it. A countryman of mine is just the man. He did a lot of just this kind of work in his own time: Marshall McLuhan.

It's fitting that McLuhan, the man who named the Global Village, should be this story's conduit. He will sweep away the religious and intellectual lard and ask the right questions, prompt relevant discussion, and generally allow us to collect new and authentic materials otherwise not available.

•

The landscape along the road to Damascus is a picturesque one. Certainly it is more temperate and pleasant than today. Instead of rotting corpses, here and there one might see copses of elegant Lebanon cedars—perhaps even an entire forest of them. The air is warm and cedar-sweet instead of being laced with cordite and the stink of wasted blood, and there are no shell-holes, no bunkers or barbed wires, no ruined villages, no hulks of burned-out Soviet or Israeli tanks, no installations of Brazilian rocket launchers.

Casement's report, along with a series of humanitarian documents written around that time, was influential, and may have created enough political pressures to have led to changes, although it should be pointed out that the discovery of extensive copper deposits in the Congo was also a factor. Eventually, a political reorganization of the region was carried out, and the massacres ended.

How does this relate to Cambodia? Well, there are differences and similarities here. The brutality is similar, the intent to exterminate is similar, and the percentage of the total population exterminated is similar.

In the Congo, however, the victims were primitive villagers, exterminated by an Imperialist European power that was ostensibly bent

Paul—or Saul as he is at this point still called—is employed by the Roman governor of Syria. His job description is something between that of a travelling judge and a freelance prosecutor and *agent provocateur*. Because he is a Greek Jew he speaks a number of languages, Greek and Hebrew foremost among them. But he is also a Roman citizen, a man of considerable hereditary privilege—and his role at this preliminary stage in his career is rather confusing to us. It was probably confusing to him.

The political climate he works in is likewise confusing to our sensibility because we have been taught to think of the past in simplistic terms. Simple it's not. The Romans hold political authority in the eastern Mediterranean by virtue of their imperial military strength. They exact crushing levels of taxation and generally sequester the bulk of the wealth, which they use to support their military ambitions and to feed the corruptions of Rome. They are a culture of pragmatists, more interested in administrative efficiency and the accumulation of personal power and wealth than in making their subject-cultures over in the Roman image. The real cultural conflict in this part of the world doesn't directly concern them. It is between Hellenistic and Judaic culture.

The ancient Jews are patrifocally tribal, monotheistic, exclusive and paranoid. In their minds, all events in the world derive from the Divinity. In our vulgarity we tend to think of the Judaic god in simple generic terms, but to the Jews, he is

---

on bringing progress and civilization to the darkness while gathering up some profits. However shocking, it is recognizable as a structurally conventional Imperialist action—one that got out of hand. If Conrad's depiction of the events is accurate, the Imperial apparatus became spooked by the primitive violence of the region and decided to wipe it out.

But in Cambodia, the opposite motives were operating. The Khmer Rouge were attempting to return to the primitive, and they tried to exterminate all vestiges of an advanced civilization that had rained down an incomprehensible flood of technological violence upon them.

In both instances, the intent was to exterminate an aspect of human consciousness. And in both instances, no restraints—certainly not

the One God among many false ones, Yahweh. And in the minds of the Jews, Yahweh is interested strictly in Jews, and in the ways in which his chosen people observe his laws. He is violent, bad-tempered, jealous and capricious. Like their god, the Jews are unfriendly to outsiders, are intolerant of foreign influences, and despise any form of exogamy—political, cultural, scientific, personal. Do not wink at their women, do not fart into a Passover crowd, and do not, above all, raise any statues in their cities.

The Greeks, who have been in the eastern Mediterranean since the time of Alexander, are pretty much the opposites of the Jews. They are cosmopolitan, casually polytheistic but open to most religious notions, including those of Judaism. On the whole, the Greeks are equally tolerant of new ideas and ancient habits, and have been practising this tolerance and curiosity all across the eastern Mediterranean world since the days of Alexander, who spread Greeks across the known world in the wake of his conquests.

Actually, these Greeks are interested in almost everything—and they are open to every exploratory, self-serving abuse. Wink at their sisters, wink at them. They will ask you to fund a statue in one of their cities, write a book or scientific treatise, make an under-the-table deal.

The personality and temperament of Paul contains elements of each and all of those contradictory Greek and Judaic characteristics. And remember, he's a Roman citizen who works

---

moral restraints—to their ultimate goals were countenanced. In a philosophical sense at least, the singleminded intent to exterminate is more important than the specific brutalities they unleashed, the barbarism they stretched the limits of. The dead cannot be brought back to life, and the re-enactment of brutality, even in an an attempt to understand or expiate it, now carries severe dangers. One of those dangers is that the re-enactment will merely be titillating. You and I, reader, live in a culture in which the average fifteen year old has seen thousands of people die—on television, and *always for reasons of dramatic logic*. Better to focus on the issue of exterminating consciousness, because that is the everyday threat we live with.

for the Roman administration. I warned you that he was complicated.

Well, what does he do for the Romans, exactly? I'm tempted to see his work as similar to the kind G. Gordon Liddy did for Richard Nixon, or the kind that Nixon did for the American Military-Industrial Complex. Specifically, his job is to denounce anyone who might "destabilize" the Roman administration. Mostly his prosecutees have been lower class Jews, but lately he has been investigating a new sect that has been proselytizing for a strange new pacifist movement.

But let's dilate our frame of reference even further. Jewish culture is based on what Christians think of as the Old Testament, a quasi-historical document that is half record and half prophesy, with some pretty good poetry thrown in. The Jews have a terrible propensity for seeing the events in their own time in terms of what they interpret as divine instruction. In the old, nomadic days tribesmen went out into the desert, made themselves delirious with hunger or thirst or hormones, and in a state of altered consciousness, interpreted and reinterpreted their tribal baggage, believing that they were in direct contact with Yahweh while they were doing it. In contemporary anthropological terms, this is an extremely common cultural rite termed a Spirit Quest.

Some of the Judaic questors, such as Moses, returned to the tribe with a written set of rules and regulations. Others had wilder visions, and still others went out into the hills and, looking

---

3

Imagine that you are a peasant. It is the sixteenth century, and you are living in a small Northern European village. You are sitting in your village church. The building around you is already several hundred years old, constructed and decorated entirely by local craftsmen, many of whom are your relatives or ancestors. As you look around at the walls and ceilings you see painted depictions of your village's history, customs and religious beliefs. You understand what you are looking at. They are matters both casually familiar and intensely intimate.

Jesus and the Virgin Mary figure prominently. Archangels,

into the tribal camp, saw what was happening there, and saw what far-off armies were about to come thundering over the top of the hills.

Quite a few armies came over the top of those hills. Imagine a nice, normal suburb stuck beside a freeway, with the international headquarters of the Hell's Angels situated on one side of it and the training camp for the Red Army Brigade on the other. You have a picture of the geographical location of ancient Palestine. It hasn't changed much since then, but that's another subject matter.

What all this means is that the ancient Jews had good reason to be the way they were. If they hadn't been, their culture would have long since been assimilated or obliterated. Some things don't change: political paranoia is always partly rooted in material fact.

There were occasional periods of political calm in those ancient days, and such periods produced the inevitable handsome, creative, and thoroughly romanticized once and future kings such as Solomon and David. By Paul's time, however, it was strictly future. The Romans, the most powerful imperial force since Alexander the Great, occupied Palestine. And the Roman occupation must have seemed—and was—more permanent than Alexander's. Not surprisingly, about every six weeks or so one crackpot or another would spend a weekend in the desert, return with a vision, and declare himself the Messiah predicted in the prophetic texts.

---

seraphim and cherubim, the saints that guard local custom are also prominent, although generally at a slightly smaller scale than Jesus and his mother. At a slightly smaller scale yet are scenes that enact and elevate life as it is lived in the village: peasants at the harvest, craftspeople at their work.

Similarly, each one of the building's many nooks and crannies is filled with icons and sculpture: the Stations of the Cross, votary receptacles, memorabilia of dead ancestors, and again, Jesus and the Virgin.

Nothing here is what is now termed a work of art. The frescoes and sculpture are less than art, and more. Perspectives are skewed, anatomical accuracies barely approximate. Michelangelo might sneer, but to you the building and most of what is in it is beautiful. Individual

The eastern Mediterranean, particularly Palestine and Syria, was a *de facto* guerrilla war zone. From the time Herod the Great became the Roman puppet king in 39 B.C. until the massacre of the Maccabees at Masada in 73 A.D., the Jews sustained roughly a million casualties. Part of this number were victims of Roman pre-emptive strikes against suspected guerrillas or their bases of operation. The rest were killed in an ongoing series of small and large scale military actions. Another 500,000 were killed in the Roman suppression of the Bar Kochva revolt in 132 A.D.

In Paul's pragmatic view, the Romans were there to stay—a viewpoint he never altered—and he regarded the local military messiahs as dangerous clowns. Indeed, it does appear that the messiahs were invariably without organized political programs, and had few resources beyond their own addled ambitions and the Jewish dislike of any authority that did not derive from Yahweh. Some of the messiahs gained large followings amongst the oppressed population, and had to be dealt with severely. In 4 B.C., for instance, Varus, the Roman governor, captured and crucified some two thousand persons simply because he felt that one or two of them might rise to prominence and become another troublesome military messiah.

•

Such anecdotes are plentiful, and I'm sure you've got the basic

---

excellence and artistic execution are not the issue in this building, and you don't give a tinker's damn for art. You don't even know what it is. What this building provides for you is a local measure of a larger cosmology than the one you can see around you in your daily life. Its ostensible focus may be the Virgin and her Child, but you are aware that near the manger where she looks after her child is a farmer tilling his fields, or a blacksmith working at a forge—things that you see each day in the village.

Disasters and delights are also recorded here, because those are part of life. But they are placed in their correct position in the landscape, like everything else. They're in scale and in context. At the centre of the cosmology, always, is the rationale for human co-operation and

picture. This is Paul's world. As we pick up on him he's on the road to Damascus with Marshall McLuhan. It's a business trip, not a Spirit Quest. He's been a busy man lately. The messianic outbreaks have recently become epidemic, and he's personally gotten a few of these crackpots tacked up. He's good at his job. He has it done quietly and quickly. The Romans don't like messes like the one they got into over Jesus.

Paul has no idea that McLuhan is really a famous Canadian coiner of slogans and phrases. He believes that he and McLuhan are two bureaucrats on their way to Damascus, and from every appearance, that's what they seem to be. They're riding camels, actually, side by side. Marshall—we'll use his first name because Paul does—is the taller of the two. Not surprisingly, Marshall looks rather uncomfortable on his mount. He peers around himself constantly, and his long legs paw awkwardly at the primitive stirrups, occasionally scraping his camel's flanks. As they near the crest of a hill, Paul heaves a sigh, one so noticeable Marshall can't help but respond to it.

"What's up, Doc?" he asks, solicitously. "Anything you want to share with a friend?"

Paul gazes at him absently, then shakes his head. "Nothing much, Marsh. I don't know. I get tired of this fucking rigmarole."

"Which one?" Marshall queries. "You talking camels or ideas?"

Paul laughs, but it is a dry laugh, without pleasure. "No,"

---

physical labour.

Actually, your church is a memory theatre. Your own life is lodged there, provided with social purpose and grace. The universe you live in is like the structure of the church. It curves over you, calm and protective. It tells you how your ancestors lived, and it tells you how you're being asked to live, and why. It warns you of the consequences of error, and it informs you that every moment of your life is penetrated by particulars, and that each individual act has consequences. Most of all, this building tells you that you are not alone.

But your universe is changing. It has recently grown much larger. Even in your village the stories have been told of the ships that have gone out into the uncharted waters and returned crammed with exotic

he says. "It's these goddamned messiahs. Every twenty-eight days another one. Always the same: new moon, half moon, old moon, no moon. They stand up, start yakking about how they're going to cause the Romans to disappear off the face of the earth, then they pull a knife on a centurion or knock over a few stalls in the market, then they get picked up. And I'm the one who tells the patrols who to pick up."

"Hey, it isn't your fault, man. You aren't the one talking about overthrowing the government. These guys know what they're doing isn't cool."

"Yeah," Paul admits, gloomily. "I guess. Stupid fucking desert rats. They're all the same: doctrinaire, militaristic, and woefully underequipped."

Marshall pulls back on the reins of his camel. The beast doesn't halt, but Paul's does. Irritably, Marshall unhooks his left foot from the stirrup and kicks the animal on the side of its neck. That doesn't do the trick either. His camel merely turns left. He kicks it again, and this time the animal twists and lunges at him.

Paul is laughing helplessly. "Holy jumped-up Jesus," he sputters. "Can't you learn to control that stupid beast? You ride like you just discovered camels last week."

Marshall smiles slyly. "What *about* this Jesus guy," he asks. "He wasn't a run-of-the-mill messiah, now, was he?"

Paul shrugs. "I never actually met the man," he says. "That was a few years back, before my time. His cult is annoying,

---

wealth. More recently, the disciples of John Calvin have been to your village. They have preached their chilly, confusing sermons attacking the old order, accusing your church of idolatry, threatening you with visions of a god more angry and jealous than the one you have known.

The god the Calvinists talk about is hard for you to imagine, harder still to connect to daily life. He is abstract, luminous, unmediated. Each person, they have said, must establish a personal relationship with that god. The rewards, they say, will fall out materially, according to the accuracy of one's worshipful relationship to Him. All other relationships are secondary.

To reinforce the message, they will go into your church and alter

because all they do is argue with one another and write. We've nailed a few of them for preaching in the market, but they're not overtly seditious like the others. The other interesting thing is that they seem to sincerely believe their man was connected. Herod Antipater's illegitimate son, I figure. The official report says that his mother was raped by a centurion named Pantherus, but if that were the case he'd never have gotten as far as he did. The Sadducees are much too good on genealogy to buy that, and more than a few of them seem to think he was the real thing—belatedly, of course."

"What kinds of proposals are his followers making?" Marshall asks, with the same sly expression. As he speaks, his camel again begins to move forward. Paul's mount follows.

They reach the crest of the hill. On the other side is a deep valley dotted by cedar groves that thin out in size and lushness as they ascend the far slope. Paul pulls alongside Marshall, whose camel has stopped of its own volition and seems unwilling to go on.

"Are you really interested in all this?" Paul asks, gesturing in the direction of a grove several hundred yards ahead, nestled in a cleft of the slope. "Why don't we take a break over in that copse and I'll tell you what I know."

"Anything to get off this stupid camel," Marshall answers with a grin. "You look like a man with the kernel of an idea."

They direct the camels into the sheltered heart of the grove, Paul leading the way. There is a cave visible in the rocks. Paul

---

it. They will break up or burn the icons and whitewash the frescoes, so as to reinforce the new relationship with God and with the abstract light of His truth.

In their cosmology, wealth, meagre as it may be in your village, is for trading up, or for storing in banks. It is not to be savoured by lavishing it on public works, on devotional objects. God is far away—far away in his imageless imperial headquarters, counting his spiritual riches.

The Calvinists will leave you alone with your new spiritual burden. There will be no one and nothing between you and the spotlessly abstract monad and his capricious regulation of the universe. There will be only the necessity of bathing yourself in the pure sterile light of direct experience. Four hundred years later you will find yourself

dismounts, leaping lightly from the stirrup as if he's been doing it all his life, which he has. Marshall is less successful. His foot catches in the stirrup and he tumbles from the animal's back, landing on his stomach with a thump. The camel, never one to miss an opportunity, bites him on the shoulder before he can scramble clear.

Marshall pulls a short, heavy whip from a pouch behind the saddle and begins to whip the camel. Paul steps in, takes the whip from his hand and pushes him away from the animal.

"Leave it be, Marsh. It's just a dumb animal. Dumb as hell, and spiritually inert. You could beat it to a pulp without it feeling anything profound, and it probably won't even catch on that it isn't smart to bite people."

Marshall turns to gaze at Paul. "That's a very Western attitude. Interesting."

Marshall takes up the camel's tethers and yanks it toward the nearest tree. Then, stupidly, he turns his back on it as he ties the tethers around the tree trunk. Predictably, the camel instantly counterattacks, swinging its heavy head into Marshall's side and knocking him flying. He lands in a heap of stale camel dung.

Paul restrains Marshall from an escalation of hostilities. "Do you want to hear what I have to say, or do you want to beat on that camel?" he asks, rhetorically. "Go sit down, and I'll tie the damned thing up for you. Go on."

Still grumbling, Marshall sits down beneath a cedar, arranges

---

staring into a television set with a canned soft drink in your hand, wondering what you should buy with your next pay-cheque.

4

You might have noticed that this book isn't "normal" fiction. There's no plot, no dialogue, and the action is frequently off-stage, upstairs, in the past, or deferred because it is a threat to sanity and well-being. The reason for this has to do with the nature and extent of the "action". First of all, like most of the profound historical events of this century, Cambodia takes place on a scale that is at once massive and covert. Second, its brutality was and is so extreme that it is

his long legs awkwardly into the lotus position beneath his heavy robes and settles in to listen.

•

"This guy Jesus," Paul begins, "isn't like the others."

"So you say," Marshall replies, wiggling his back to straighten the robes. "But where are the differences from the run-of-the-mill messiahs you prosecute? Can you organize this data set so I can see what it carries?"

"Okay," Paul says, grinning slightly at Marshall's peculiarly imageless but metaphoric way of speaking. "Let's start with his birth. Like I said, he seems to have been connected. But it's a cockeyed connection. One side of it is laundered so white you can't see anything human, and the other side, the illegitimate side, is shrouded in layer after layer of hokey miracles.

"His mother—Apollo alone knows what kind of battered ego she must have had—is treated as nothing but a receptacle. I can't really tell how clean she was, or what she thought of it, because the followers have whitewashed her so totally.

"The father is the loose connection. That's where Antipater is lurking, if he was involved, or the centurion. The followers more or less admit that Joseph was a lame uncle, even though he seems to have brought the boy through the early years with real affection. The official line is that it was a virgin conception—Angel of Yahweh flashed her."

---

unthinkable.

Dramatizing individual episodes will not capture the essentials of Cambodia. Such an approach will inevitably distort the issues by introducing lyric elements of pathos and character that are precisely what is absent in mass reality. All the conventional tools of fiction are as inappropriate and misrepresenting as the analytical ones that Hannah Arendt used to send 25 million Africans into the ether of abstraction. A new method is needed.

This is disturbing to me for a number of reasons. One of them is that I have a deep respect for the traditions of literature. I've traced those traditions back as far as Gilgamesh, and the one thing I've found to be a constant among great writers is that they have taken on the

"It sounds pretty low-density," Marshall comments.

"Well, it is, and then again it isn't. Actually I'm kind of impressed with the way the central group works it. It's almost beautiful, because it covers everything up, no matter what the genealogy really is, and the only way a convert can question it is to doubt the word and the miracle of Yahweh, as it were."

"Explain."

"The central group operates by committee, citing some remark the Messiah made about them being the sole conduit of divine information after his transmogrification."

"His what?"

"After the Romans crucified him some odd things happened. Or so it's claimed. The central committee—the disciples—and some of the other insiders say that he came back to life for a while. Rose from the Dead, like. He's supposed to have preached a few sermons and then disappeared. The official line is that he ascended to Yahweh from the top of some mountain."

"I heard he took off with this reformed hooker he married, and headed west by boat."

"Yeah," Paul admits. "I've heard that story, too. But who cares where he went and why? What's interesting is what he left behind."

"And that is?"

Paul stares off toward the distant hills. "Okay," he says, after a moment of speculation. "Here's how I see it. The first important remainder is the idea of a controllable—or at least

---

most difficult subject matter presented by the time they lived in—enacted it, dramatized it, embodied it.

That should be comforting, but it isn't. No one wants Cambodia re-enacted, certainly not for the sake of artistic expression. To do so would be ghoulish, and besides, I'm not really here to express myself. More important, re-enacting Cambodia would answer few of the questions raised by it.

Hence, I'm going to define my terms and explain what I think is at stake, even though all my training as an artist tells me to play the game and convince by art, not by reason.

The trouble with playing the old game of art is that art is no longer a game. The rule book has been burned. As recently as a hundred

accessible—divine energy, as embodied initially by Jesus and secondarily by his disciples. They're calling it the Holy Spirit or the Holy Ghost. What they call it doesn't matter. What's important is that it gives Yahweh a mediated presence in the corporeal world. Intangible, but mediated. And rationally accessible.''

"Isn't that just another internecine attempt to interrupt Pharisaic civil hegemonies?''

"Not on the surface. They're respectfully Judaic, but with a subtle difference. It puts the civil interpretative authority in the hands of a very small group. It's the compactness of the interpretative authority that's new. They probably started off by objecting to Pharisaic power, but that doesn't matter. So what if it's an accident.''

"Never thought of it that way,'' Marshall admits. "You're right. But I'm still unclear about the operational difference between the apostles and the other sects and factions that are claiming a link to Jesus. The apostles have been around longer, and they were personal friends or relatives, but that's all.''

"They're different, all right. For one thing, most of them write, or have the wealth to allow them to hire scholars. Most of them are working on different versions of a biography, and they're clearly collaborating. From what I've seen it amounts to a pretty cohesive and rational depiction of the events.''

"My understanding is that pretty well every faction is working on a biography.''

---

years ago artists knew and respected the rules, and so did the public. And by "the public'' I mean all those members of society with full citizenship rights and duties. I do not mean the voluntary public that almost all art today takes as its audience.

Somewhere along the line, the old forms of artistic expression— writing, painting, music—those with techniques deeply lodged in thought and physical research and with aims that were creative in the educative or legislative sense—were separated from the public realm. They have since been placed in a kind of reservation where the artists are encouraged, or forced, to chose between entertaining their patrons in increasingly vulgar ways or educating voluntary "clients'', often in government-funded agencies like the universities or art galleries.

"True, but also untrue. Each of the cult's factions does seem to write a lot. I've had some of my agents confiscate texts. Most of the ones I've seen are pretty bizarre. A lot of repressed political/sexual material, and the predictable desert music. Some of it is marginally seditious, and some of it is prosecutable."

"But the inner group isn't seditious?"

"Oh, anything can be made to appear seditious," Paul says, with a cynical laugh. "But these guys are quite slick. Their trick is to be carefully non-violent. They acknowledge Roman corporeal powers—or seem to—and then ignore them in favour of rules for personal conduct that they say act as a conduit to their Kingdom of Heaven."

Marshall stands up, obviously stimulated by what he is hearing. "Shit," he says. "This is exciting. A whole civilization of personal universes, a cybernetwork directly linked to the cosmos and the divinity. It's ahead of its time, but it has fantastic possibilities. Particularly if all the linkups are kept opaque."

Paul isn't listening. He isn't watching, either. If he had been, he would have noticed Marshall's pacings taking him dangerously close to the camels, and that Marshall's animal is subtly edging toward his friend's radius. If he'd been watching, he would have seen his companion stop close to the camels with his back turned. In fact, Paul seems to have gone into a trance.

The conscienceless camel makes its move. It swings its long neck against Marshall's shoulder, bouncing him against a cedar

---

This has taken place in a political context in which a key right of democratic citizenship is the right to be ignorant.

Games don't work well unless they have rules that the participants understand and agree to honour. In its retreat from the public realm, art has lost its rule book. The moral discipline still survives, but only for a minority of practising artists and fewer still of their clients. The subject matter of most art is now limited and trivial, and most artists now operate as entrepreneurs of the topical. The reasons for their public successes and failures are almost identical to the reasons business entrepreneurs succeed or fail—accurate market location and fashion have replaced relevance and utility. For the vast majority of art clients, art is just another decorative or entertaining commodity—an

tree. Marshall's skull raps off the trunk with a sickening crunch, and he crumples in a heap, unconscious. A camel hoof thuds against his ribs, and the animal begins to twist on its tethers so as to be able to finish the job.

The shuffling breaks Paul's concentration. He looks up, recognizes what is about to happen, and in one movement scoops up the whip and swings it at the camel's backing hindquarters, saving Marshall from having his skull crushed into splinters. Paul pulls him clear. For several long minutes Marshall lies slumped against a cedar, unconscious.

Paul is upset. It isn't so much the near-fatal incident with the camel that upsets him as it is the metaphor proposed by it: all life is violence. One act of violence begets a second, and the reprisals go on to infinity. Trying to avoid the thought, Paul scans the far slopes with careful attention. Probably there are bandits over there too, somewhere. In some stupid cave, living on rat meat and insects, all in the name of hatred and ambition.

He feels a sudden rush of desperation. It's a treadmill he's on, a treadmill that seems to be constantly speeding up. Rome on one side, and Jerusalem on the other. There *must* be an alternative.

•

When Marshall opens his eyes, there are walls around him. For a split second he is confused, but then he realizes that they're

---

adjunct to one's personal style, a signal of sophistication and good taste that never demands to be tested in action.

This is no Rodney Dangerfield complaint. There's more at stake than my personal dignity or the general dignity of artists. Economics and culture are again collapsing into one another, and artistic forms are being challenged to either account for their existence on a functional basis, or to disappear. In the abstract, that is refreshing; almost good news. But an electronically technologized civilization that encourages ignorance is involved, one in which human motivations are as easily manufactured as a mousetrap. Citizens and artists alike are the mice.

•

inside a real cave, and that Paul has dragged him there. Paul is a few feet away, sitting with his back propped against a large stone. He's built a small fire, and is watching the shadows flicker across the stained rock. Still groggy, Marshall registers the tableau. It has a familiarity that he senses is significant, but in his dazed condition it doesn't register. Experimentally, he massages his ribs. Other remembered images and ideas enter, and the pinball mental activity he loves takes over.

Encouraged, he tries to stand, but slumps back dizzily. His head is throbbing about equally from the ideas that are pinging to and fro and from the whacking the camel gave him.

"Goddamned stupid camel," he mutters aloud.

Paul looks up. "What's that?"

Marshall grins lamely. "Nothing, really. I was just thinking."

"You were the one who walked in front of the camel. You have a disorderly mind."

"Unlike you, right?"

"I don't walk in front of vicious camels, if that's what you mean."

"If you were really smart you wouldn't be prosecuting your own people on behalf of a bunch of wine-worshipping kooks."

"The Romans keep order," Paul says, primly.

"There's a better way to do that, believe me."

"How's that?" Paul asks, suddenly focused and serious.

"You change the rules of the game. You invent something that nobody has ever seen before, or you take over something

---

Let me formally introduce a metaphor I've already used several times. It is the metaphor of the Imperium—the golden, distant city where the stakes are not quite personal but are always ultimate, where what is truthful and good receives its apotheosis and dissemination—or its suppression. Every major epoch has, sooner or later, created its imperial centres: Jerusalem, Carthage, Athens and Rome for the ancient world; London, Paris, New York and Moscow for the modern world.

The chief promise of the post-modern world, the world that began to take shape after 1945 and which became a reality in about 1975, is that the mass media of film and television and the more recent media of computer technology would decentralize the Imperium, scattering

that already exists and renovate it."

"Like what, for instance?"

"Like this Jesus business. Sure, the guy was a little off the wall. But he had some great ideas. Get in on the ground floor and rework them. I hear they've got an opening for an apostle."

Paul laughs, but there's no bitterness in the laughter. Until the moment he saved Marshall from the camel it had never occurred to him that Roman authority wasn't functioning well, or that there might be an alternative or adjunct to it.

As if reading his thoughts, Marshall continues. "The trouble with the Romans is that they're visible. A really successful kind of authority is invisible and internalized, like Yahweh. You've got a whole damned civilization looking for an alternative to existing institutions—spiritual or political."

"Don't use the word *spiritual*," Paul says irritably.

"Why not? The realm of spirit is just the interface between authority and those subject to the authority."

"Don't use the word *interface*, either."

Marshall rolls his eyes. He likes Paul, but often finds him too fixed on his temporal authority role. Power is seductive, Marshall says to himself. But once you've been seduced and laid, you've got to live with it. Better to be the seducer. And he senses that Paul might seduce the entire future if he can be nudged into a slightly different direction. He, Marshall, is here to witness the nudge—perhaps to administer it. What an opportunity!

---

it and its manna across the planet electronically. This New World promised to spread undreamed-of economic and cultural wealth on an equitable, democratic basis. All humanity would have the same right to consume its products.

The formal announcement, for those who are comforted by historical events, names and dates, was almost certainly the publication in 1964 of Marshall McLuhan's *Understanding Media*, which began to popularize the metaphor of the Global Village. So no reader will be confused about where I stand, let me declare my hostility to the effects and practices of the Global Village.

There is no sense in expressing hostility to the concept of the Global Village. It is already fact, and literally everyone on this planet is going

52

He decides to lay it on as straight as he can. "Never mind my language," he says, "I have a vision of the future you'll find interesting."

Paul laughs. "Hey, man," he says. "Just because you get kicked by a camel doesn't mean you should start having visions of the future. Be smart. Remember what I do to people who have visions of the future."

Marshall experiences a moment of uncertainty. He isn't sure whether Paul is serious or not. He plunges on anyway. "You be smart. The content of visions isn't what matters. We both know what the visions all say—'A military prince will come to destroy the nations'. 'Babylon will be inhabited strictly by owls', and 'from the military prince will come a kingdom that will not be destroyed'. Why don't we sit down and translate all that into operable terms?"

"Go ahead," Paul says, getting to his feet and moving to the mouth of the cave.

Marshall brushes past him, and begins pacing back and forth once more, this time staying well clear of the camel. Paul notes that the camel is glaring at Marshall with its lips peeled back in a snarl.

"Well," Marshall begins, "the first thing we do is forget the overt messages. A political revolution can't be accomplished here, not in an immediate and military sense. You know the Romans. They're not going to be defeated by a bunch of desert-crazed guerrillas, or urban ones crazed by the marketplace. The

---

to have to come to terms with what it is doing to human consciousness and political practices. We may complain about what it does to us as individuals, and we may mourn the passing of a world that might seem to be more simple and direct. But while we do that, some of us will employ its technological adjuncts. I do, for one.

Complaining about the shallowness of the Global Village, mourning the lost paradise of the old world, or using the new technological advantages will not make much of a difference, either to the fate of the planet or to what goes on in this story. What does matter is the degree to which we understand what the Global Village means, how it has created a new Imperium for the post-modern world, and what that Imperium will take away from us if we do not defend ourselves

Romans have no aversion to violence. It's their medium, just like exogamy is for the Greeks, and endogamy for the Jews. And all media are self-fulfilling. They reproduce the medium first, ultimately, and as a controlling content of all incidental events in between."

Paul nods and a sly smile touches the corners of his mouth. "But between the medium and the message is the business."

"Exactly. The business of staying alive—eating, sleeping, getting laid, and so on. That's where your opportunity lies. Translate those prophetic visions into business terms and you'll see what I mean."

Paul scratches his head. It is a gesture of calculation, not of confusion. "A prince will come to control the enemy nations," he says, almost under his breath.

"Right. Now forget about the owls. All that means is that all autocratic political power is temporary and expedient, if not in a single lifetime, then over the long term. Even Rome will collapse someday."

"Out of the manipulation of political structure will come an administrative technique that will transcend temporal power. Son of a bitch!"

"You're getting it. Now have another look at your pal Jesus and his apostles. What they created, unknowingly, is a potentially perfect administrative system. First off, it posits no direct ideological threat to Rome or to the Judaic Establishment. As the numbers of converts grows it will become one, but even

---

and our planet against it. Why? I'm going to argue that Cambodia is the subtext of the Global Village, and that the Global Village has had its purest apotheosis yet in Cambodia.

The Global Village has done almost nothing it claimed it would do. There has been no redistribution of economic and cultural wealth. Economically, the Third World has become poorer, particularly the bottom half. In some of those Third World countries, a wealthy upper middle class has emerged or has become more wealthy. And in the industrialized world, the shift in wealth upward has been accelerating just as rapidly, if less visibly. The working classes of the industrialized world, bemused by vast increases in their disposable income, do not seem to have noticed the quantities of consumer items that have come

that could be made to seem elusive. Particularly if you adjust the data coming from the figurehead. Happily, the subject in question is dead, and so he won't be making any more radical pronouncements or attacking the banking system."

"I've got it. I can take it over by creating an administrative apparatus that secures the central committee as a spiritual corporate body. Then I can franchise out the conversions and work out all the housekeeping procedures as I go. And the workers get the Kingdom of Heaven and proximity to the Holy Ghost. No expenditure of power or funds."

Marshall's smile deepens. "It's a unique opportunity you've got on your hands," he says. "You won't see it come to fruition in your lifetime, but I can absolutely guarantee that in a hundred years your faction will have effectively wiped out the internal dissent, and in three hundred, you'll have Rome. And you'll be in firm control of the apparatus within your own lifetime. The other apostles will get direct memory and the Prophet. That's what they'll want, being as conservative as you say they are. But you'll control the medium and you'll get the profits."

Paul winces. "That's a disgusting pun, Marsh," he says.

"I never could resist a pun."

Paul relaxes against a cedar. Across the valley, he detects movement, or thinks he does. He looks again, and decides it is merely the sun raising heat waves from the distant forest. He stretches wide his arms, and gazes up into the face of the

---

to be classified as necessities and have become indispensible to full citizenship.

For almost everyone, life continues to be violent. In fact, its violence is increasing. Far more human beings have been massacred or have starved in the 70s and 80s than in the 50s and 60s.

It is likewise difficult to argue that anyone, anywhere, has benefitted culturally, unless one is prepared to say that Afghani refugees in the slums of Karachi listening to Michael Jackson or Saudi tribesmen watching *Dallas* on portable television sets in the middle of the desert is a cultural advance. All we've seen is a centralization of the sources and distribution of culture.

In my own country, Canada, people all across the north, including

sun. The glare momentarily blinds him. When he looks back at the cedars, he can see nothing at all, nothing but the future he will make.

One of the camels groans and begins to shuffle nervously on its tether. Paul looks to see if his friend is in danger, but with his vision now clear, he discovers that he is alone.

---

aboriginal Indians and Eskimos, can relieve their isolation with as many as seventy television channels through satellite receiving technology. Isn't that wonderful? Now they can be interested in the same things urban people in Atlanta or Detroit or Los Angeles are manipulated into being interested in.

McLuhan, for all his glib brilliance, didn't understand that the Global Village was going to be Los Angeles, where the majority of television programming originates. Nor did he understand what every amateur computer programmer knows: that the quality of information produced by electronic systems is totally dependent on the quality of information originally provided to them, and on the quality and intention of the data processing. On the one hand, garbage in, garbage

Universal Chicken

You've just pulled your car off the freeway into one of those new service station complexes. You've been driving since dawn. You're tired, the car needs gas, and you're mildly hungry. It's just past noon, one of those horrible days that seem more frequent now than they used to be—no sun, no rain, just dull cloud from horizon to horizon—like having no weather at all.

As you coast up to the pumps, stop, and shut off the motor, you experience a sense of unreality. You can't remember where you are. You look around you, but that's no help. You still don't know where you are because there's nothing here you haven't seen somewhere else. Your entire body is numb from sitting in the car, from your toes to your ass right up to your brain. For a moment you suspect there's an exhaust leak and you've been bonked by carbon monoxide. Then you realize that the poison that has gotten you is of a different dispensation.

Your mind is worse off than the rest of you. It's utterly entangled in bizarre patterns of iconographic images: Gulf, Pepsi, Speedy Muffler King, Burger King. You must have seen

---

out. On the other, the narrower the interpretative conduit and the larger the flow of information, the more absolutely the law of the lowest common denominator applies.

No one, anywhere, predicted the emergence of franchise-oriented consumer capitalism, and certainly no one has calculated the economic effects it has had and will continue to have in the future. Marxist economists operate in a state of either bewilderment or nostalgia, and the economists of the Right and Centre are too busy gloating over the rubble it has made of the enemy's theoretical base to have noticed that it is shaking the structure of capitalist economies apart by both removing the cream of local profits from the communities that create them and destroying local initiative and particularities.

twenty or thirty sets of Golden Arches since you started driving this morning. Yet you can't quite focus on what it is you've been taking in, because your ability to connect one thought to another, and to formulate the words that build them, seems to have been replaced by an unpleasant buzzing in your head. You shake yourself, as if to unlock the aphasia, and the motion allows you to glimpse, for just a second, what has caused it.

All morning you've been driving through a kind of anti-memory device. In the Middle Ages they called memory devices "theatres". They were mental landscapes that helped people to remember who they were, what and where they were, and what connected them to other people, to nature and to God. What you've been in is the opposite. There are no gods, no nature if it can be tarmacked, and the people you see are encapsulated the same way you are inside cars or consumer identities. The anti-memory device keeps pounding images into your head that tell you what to buy or what's fashionable. And while it's doing that it wears away your sense of who you are, where you are and where you're going by convincing you that you're just like everyone else and that all places are the same.

It's *Planet of the Franchises* they're putting you in, and the images you see are for product outlets: everything from places to sleep, to food, to gasoline and parts for your car. But you're not responding the way you're supposed to. You feel a craving for something is singular, something slightly inefficient, something that has no head office and no profit-taking

---

Yet franchise capitalism shouldn't be such a surprise. Like the rest of the apparatus of our commoditized society, it has its spiritual roots in Platonist doctrine, and in the Calvinist practice of that doctrine; it is the logical result of the coupling of monopoly capitalism and bourgeois ideology. In North America, it has an added dimension. It returns us to the impulse that settled the continent in the first place: Queen Isabella did not send Christopher Columbus on a voyage of discovery, she gave him a franchise that demanded that he exploit what he discovered for the mercantile gain of the franchise owner. In the new world, God would reward wealth, not understanding. It was exploited without ever being explored.

The interpreters of culture are no better off than the defenders of

trajectory—something, anything that is solely and only *where* you see it. You've seen so little particularity this morning that an anaesthetized sector of your mind actually questions your craving for it.

The villain, you decide, shaking off the self-doubting question, is the freeway. No, it's larger than that. The villain is wraparound North America. And you understand, with a helpless sensation, that it is closing in on you and on this small planet.

Every day now it gets worse. More total. When you pull into a motel tonight, you will probably fall asleep watching the same television spectacles that merchandise millions of other people into temporary oblivion after a full day of being assaulted by the franchise products that have been assaulting you all morning. It's a subtle assault, of course. At least until you recognize that you're being colonized and controlled by it.

You're told that this is the new wave of democracy—everybody gets to have the same variety of products. Somehow, the commonality of it isn't very comforting. Isn't democracy supposed to be built on differences and a respect for those differences—the more the merrier? Being one of "The People" doesn't send the chill up your spine it once did. The only things you can share with your fellow citizens these days are consumer preferences. Once, you remember, you shared a similarity of values and an outlook toward life and experience. Or maybe you just thought you did. Whatever it was, this world you've

---

local custom. As the press and media become increasingly centralized in ownership and editorial orientation, cultural commentators are quietly being disappeared or reduced to the governance of unimportant amateurisms. Mass media has become synonymous with either vulgarity or intellectual mediocrity. It is even becoming smug about it, cynically pointing out that the public is getting what the public has "demanded".

Artists have responded to this in two ways. Many have retreated (as they did during the Reformation) to the seclusion of the universities, hiding their interest in particularity within an ugly hybrid of antiquarian formalism, traditional scholarship, and the residual apparatus of our fast-decaying liberalism—academic tenure and the

seen today is one that isn't shareable. And it can't be experienced. Experience is a two-way process; you affect what affects you. That's how democracy is supposed to function. But if you try to affect your television set or your Big Mac, it doesn't work. You can only consume or refuse those things. Anti-democracy, anti-memory.

There you go, right? You're not even out of the car and already you're ranting. A wry grin crosses your face. Your family and most of your friends accuse you of always having to criticize something. Lighten up, they say. You think too damned much.

Mostly you've felt proud to be spoken of that way. But today, thinking is a burden. It was always the singularity of the material world that made thinking pleasurable, and here there's nothing of that to attach a thought to. Instead, there's the freeway behind you and in front of you, and there are the franchises: boing, boing, blip, blip.

Your logical allies—the architects, planners, university theoreticians, the anarchist avant-garde—aren't much comfort. They seem to want the world cleared of uncontrolled singularities just as much as the corporate accountants and ad men who are perpetrating this desert. They all want to see a billion self-motile universes, each in its own sealed-off vacuum. You curse your allies for giving up, but they just sneer and accuse you of being a dinosaur.

•

---

flimsy logic of academic freedom. Others, embracing the entrepreneurial élan of the marketplace, divest themselves of all particularity, abandon investigation of formal properties and possibilities, and serve up what they hope the market will find attractive.

Having recognized what is happening to art, I'm going to make an absurd gesture. I propose that the subject of alternatives to the small and shrinking plot of barren territory assigned to artists within this new Imperium called the Global Village be opened. Without denying the immense effectiveness of electronic communications, and with full knowledge that as a print-oriented artist I am quite possibly a dinosaur, let me take the position that survival of the body is not the ultimate goal of life—not personal survival nor the survival of the

A uniformed attendant is advancing toward your car with a friendly franchise grin on his face. You climb out of the car and turn your back to him, stretching your cramped muscles as you tell him neutrally to fill up the tank. Then you lumber in the direction of the main building of the complex, half-wishing that you were Tyrannosaurus Rex but understanding that you're rather less than that. You're one of those nameless duck-billed herbivore dinos without teeth, and you're probably looking for a quiet pond full of lily pads to munch on. You're depressed and you're depressing. You might as well get into the role.

You've stopped here because there's a restaurant in the complex, and you walk to the restaurant door, open it, and step inside. In the last few days you've seen this restaurant at a dozen places along the freeway. You even know what's on the menu, but when you sit down at one of the tables, you ask to see one anyway, because you're an optimistic dinosaur.

No luck. You reluctantly order a dish that consists of blobs of dessicated chicken pressed into uniform lumps and deep fried. Chicken Delights, they call them. Or NuggetzaChicken, Chicken Strips. Who cares what they call it. It's Universal Chicken.

The chickens you'll be eating died months ago thousands of miles away in an anonymous processing plant. The birds were raised in commercial grow-pens without ever seeing the light of day. When they reached the appropriate size and weight they were thrown, machine-gutted but still twitching, into a vat of

---

existing body of forms that are accepted as the structural bases for written literature. Let the old ways die. And if art and artists are not to disappear with them, they had better be prepared to commit piracy on any technique that will float and carry content.

This is an essay, a short story, a novella, a harangue, a poem, a rant—whatever is dictated by the necessities of my subject matter. That puts me in the jungle, as an insurgent and as a guerrilla. No, I am not trying to gather dignity to my efforts. The subject matter is Cambodia, where all dignity has been rendered obsolete.

■

acid that dissolved the feathers and loosened the bones. Then the carcasses were ripped apart in a huge machine that separates flesh from bone with remarkable speed and efficiency. Your dog may be eating the guts right now in your kitchen at home, and the fertilizer made from the reconstituted bones and feathers is probably on a boat headed for a Third World country. Or something equally dechickenizing and gloomy.

You smile gloomily at the witticism, and you smile gloomily at the waitress as she tells you, with some pride, that your chicken will take less than five minutes to prepare. You're not impressed. You know how it's done. Each pre-packaged portion will be taken fresh from the freezer and dropped into a boiling mixture of deodorized pre-processed beef fat and oil pressed from peanuts or rapeseed. Those identities also obliterated.

You look around for the washroom. You'll have enough time to pee and to wash up before the chicken arrives. Good. There it is.

But as you approach the washroom door, a tall burly man wearing a mackinaw coat intersects your path. He seems to be angry about something, and for a moment you wonder irrationally if he's going to beat the shit out of you. Maybe he's one of those whacked out ex-marines you've read about. Or maybe he's been reading your mind and he's decided that he doesn't have to stand for your depressing crap. Or maybe it's just that you're a stranger. You make a swift defensive

---

As soon as the last anti-Khmer Rouge resistance collapsed in the urban centres of Cambodia in 1975, the Khmer Rouge evacuated these centres, with considerable brutality and loss of life. The refugee-swollen populations were forced into the countryside, ostensibly to work on agricultural projects that would allow the battered country to feed itself. Phnom Penh, the largest of the cities with at least a million refugees, was transformed into a ghost town in a matter of days after the "liberation"

The Khmer Rouge then painted over, with white paint, every single sign in the city. There has never been even a remotely adequate explanation for why this was done, except to note it as a curiosity of Khmer Rouge barbarism, or to say that an apparently irrational

calculation: the man is a little bigger than you are, but you're younger, and from the look of it, in better shape despite the awful day you've been having.

He doesn't attack. Like you, he simply needs to pee. Quite badly, you decide, when he shoulders in front of you and slams open the washroom door. There are two urinals in the washroom, and you're soon standing shoulder to shoulder with him as both of you unzip. Perhaps it is the commonality of your intention that causes it. Whatever it is, neither one of you can go.

Actually, you know why. There's a strange phenomenon that sometimes occurs when men use a public urinal. It derives from a very simple visual principle: an object viewed from directly above appears smaller than it actually is. This quirk of human visual perception has been the source of all kinds of idiotic male behaviour. *Everyone has a larger one than you have.*

Some men respond by becoming violent. That's why so many bar fights start in the vicinity of the men's washroom. Other men, however, are able to suppress the instinctive resort to violence. They simply freeze. That's what you usually do. And that's what you do here.

The only parts of you that freeze are your bladder and the small circuit in your brain that unlocks the bladder. The rest of you is doing just great. In fact, it's operating at twice its normal rate. You're twitchy in at least thirty locations, none of which you are willing to scratch right now. For two or three seconds you refuse to let it get to you. But you're up against

---

order was given, and the order was carried out—one among many. I have a different theory. Perhaps, like the Calvinist zealots of the sixteenth and seventeenth centuries who painted over the muralled churches, they wanted to obliterate particularity, direction and local memory, creating in its stead a single focus on the monadic truth, the City of God.

This city, emptied of all but cold ideology and the lethal bureaucracy that accompanied it, then began to obliterate the identities of Cambodians in the name of efficiency, simplicity and purity. I would like you, my readers, to consider that, in a less direct and violent way, the Global Village is doing the same thing to us.

history and biology together, and no matter how you struggle to outsmart yourself, you can't go.

Naturally, the guy next to you always knows about your struggle, and is laughing at you, quietly but contemptuously. He empties his own bladder without a hitch while you listen and squirm. As he leaves, you must bear his snigger of derision.

But this time, the guy next to you, despite his mackinaw and his marine training, isn't doing any of those things. The two of you stand shoulder to shoulder as the seconds tick by, vibrating like irrigation systems with airlocks in their pipes. It becomes a race to see which one will be able to go first, and you both stay in position, straining absurdly, the veins in your necks and foreheads swelling with the effort.

Nothing doing. You're stuck. But your competitor isn't doing any better, and the situation strikes you as funny. This is, of course, partly tactics. If you can relax enough to laugh, you might be able to break the freeze. On the other hand, if you laugh too hard, you risk peeing on the wall, or on your competitor, or worst of all, you risk causing him to think that you are laughing at him and his self-perceived undersized equipment.

You therefore marshal all your will and cunning, and laugh for yourself alone, silently. No dice. You still can't go. The elusive triggering mechanism is up there in your head somewhere, like it has been since you were a small boy. It's making fun of you, actually. But hey, you're not a small boy anymore. You're a man. You don't believe in the game it is

---

5

Angkor Wat, the complex of stone temples built in Northern Cambodia between the ninth and thirteenth centuries by the original Khmer monarchs, was rediscovered only in the nineteenth century, and rescued from the jungles largely in this century. For Westerners, the complex is a disturbing legacy, partly because of the constant struggle that must be waged to prevent the jungle from taking back what has been reclaimed, and partly because of the alien nature of the ruins.

The nature of the political energy that created the long-dead Khmer civilization is as alien and obscure as the artistic energies that provide Angkor Wat with its affective powers. We know that for three or four

playing with you, for Christ's sake, and with a wild burst of mature and non-sexual energy, you quit the game. You simply walk away from it and from the urinal. To hell with it. You zip up your fly, and leave the other guy standing there, still straining. You move to the sink, wash and dry your hands and stroll out the door. You're feeling truly adult and in control. You didn't need to pee in the first place. You may never have to pee again.

You return to your table and sit down, still sure of yourself. Right on cue the waitress appears with the Universal Chicken. It looks just as it did when you had it in Seattle or Winnipeg or Akron, Ohio. It tastes so bland you feel more like you're taking on fuel than eating.

Ahah! That's exactly what the fiends who invented Universal Chicken want to make you feel like. They are trying to convince you that you're no different from a machine, an automobile. That's what this whole goddamned complex is designed for. You're no dinosaur to these people, you're a 1956 Buick. The bastards find some way to turn you into a mechanical device of one sort or another at least a dozen times a day. And in that gloomy future you're driving toward, the self-conscious mental activities you engage in to defend yourself will probably be thought as irrelevant as fins on a car. Or as subversive. If they aren't both of those already. Probably the computer police are piling up secret dossiers on disaffected consumers like you. Consumer cynicism, like free memory, is too capricious and

---

hundred years the Khmers rose out of the tangle of jungle and flourished. During that time Khmer stonemasons carved their stylized shapes from the jungle stone in praise of their imported Hindu gods Brahma, Vishnu and Shiva, integrating them into a host of older local deities, animal and ancestral. Then the jungle closed in once more.

Angkor Wat is a site of symmetrical beauty and wonder, but the wonderment it evokes is not the same kind as that evoked by the pyramids of Egypt. The mystery of these stones is not with how they were carved and placed together, or with why—as with the pyramids. There is little at Angkor Wat that articulates the mysteries of death and rebirth, nor are the temples tied to the cycle of the seasons or, as in Egypt, the passages of a great river. The temples are simply there,

anarchic. Those who are infected by it are enemies of self-management, socio/economic organization, and the auto industry. God, you're boring.

That last thought turns what began as a polite dinner argument you were having with yourself into an ugly brawl. You begin to toy with the blobs of Universal Chicken. Look, you say, pushing one of them to the centre of the plate, they're after everything that isn't standardized. They want to break you down because uniqueness is a neural stimulus. It makes people think. Instead of having order neatly externalized (and therefore manageable), free-thinking human beings create weird internal habits and clarities that make them inefficient consumers of merchandise. And you, you're the worst sort. The only things you enjoy are those that are somehow substandard and screwed up. You only like apples with spots on them, you like wackos too much. You prefer poor service and winding country roads. You're going nowhere.

Sure. That's why you're here, sitting in this service station restaurant partaking of the homogenized, blenderized humiliation of materiality. The deep-fried turds of Universal Chicken in front of you are unrecognizable except as a slick new variety of primeval animal soup. And you're gobbling them up like the rest of the consuming suckers. Some threat you are.

You finish that thought and your second-last piece of Universal Chicken at the same time. You're now in a state of near-suicidal despair, and you're looking for some way to fight

---

with their monkeys and vines and leeches, as arbitrary and silent as the imported gods the Khmers worshipped, perverse in their cratered persistence.

One wonders what thoughts went through the minds of the stonemasons as they carried out the orders of their masters. Did they take pleasure in creating the intricate filigree of stone spires? The gods of Angkor Wat are at once geometric and sensual, the stone animals and human figures nightmarish. All are curiously static, as if the stonemasons sensed the jungle waiting to move back in. The cosmology evoked seems to exude control, but it is the kind of control that is unsupported by any sense of order save that of the inevitability of death and decay.

back against this overwhelming conspiracy to remove your imagination and your will. All you can manage is to refuse to eat the last piece.

You push it off your plate, poke it across the table and onto the floor. When you look up, satisfied with your small act of protest, the waitress is gazing at you with a puzzled expression. You ignore her, and your eyes search the restaurant once more for some missed particularity—anything single and unique will do: a cracked window, a flaw in the plaster, anything at all.

There's nothing. The waitresses are uniformed, the pump-jockeys are uniformed, the whole place is designed to create dull familiarity. Every damned thing you can see in this scene is empty, except your gas tank and your stomach. And, ahah! your bladder.

Your private argument with yourself has shifted the stresses, and you feel a sudden urgent pressure. You pay the bill, pocket the receipt, and swing through the washroom door, ready to unzip and let fly in the same motion.

The guy in the mackinaw is still standing at the urinal.

A wave of delight passes through you, sweeping your gloom away in an instant. In fact, it is so profound that you nearly lose control of your bladder. You move in next to him, stifling a giggle. You chance a peek at him, and see that he's exhausted, his face lined with now-epic tension and effort. He turns to look at you, his eyes filled with shame and utter hopelessness, and you are overcome by compassion for him. For the first time

---

The chief emotions Angkor Wat has produced in Western visitors are pathos and dread. The temples and statues, scarred by the centuries and celebrated only by the elements and the jungle, seem direct testimony to the mortality of human ambition. Angkor Wat does not celebrate the human ingenuity that built it, and the temples and statues seem to offer no opinion on the human capacity for order and harmony. The tangle of the ever-encroaching jungle vines is the only constant message.

The Bayon, the last great complex of monuments, is a series of repetitive and abstract statues of Lokeshvara, the grinning Bodhisattva. This figure delivers Angkor Wat's most eloquently chilling message. Visitors are frequently disturbed by the joyless silence of the Bayon.

in your life, you are able to speak to another man while standing at a urinal.

"Lousy out there, eh?" you say, staring carefully at the wall in front of you.

Before he can reply, you let fly, and, unable to suppress your sense of well-being, you turn to your companion and grin right in his face. Damn the consequences.

With a groan of relief, he too begins to pee. He smiles back at you gratefully. After all, you've saved him from the unspeakable fate of having to spend the rest of his life standing in front of a washroom urinal in the middle of nowhere. Then, as sweet relief returns him to normal consciousness, he returns his gaze to the wall.

"Yeah," he replies coldly. "It's a pisser."

Lokeshvara's grin, they say, is rictal, the grin that pain and suffering paints across the face of the dead and dying.

∎

The Khmer Rouge regime of 1975-1979 consciously attempted to return Cambodia to the mysteries of Lokeshvara, and to the glories of Angkor Wat. In order to accomplish this, they tried to change both word and world. Prior to the Khmer Rouge coming to power, the Cambodian word for revolution had a conventional meaning: *Bambah-bambor*—"uprising", "reconstruction". Under Pol Pot's regime, the word for revolution became *pativattana*: "return to the past". The

The Hinton Body Bag

I'm a cameraman for network television news, Pacific Region. A while back, just after Christmas if I remember correctly, there was a train wreck up in Northwestern Alberta. A freight train didn't make a stop off-track and as a result, it collided head-on with a passenger train. They're still arguing about why it happened. That's standard procedure. The government is investigating, but the railway is publicly owned, so it's hardly going to be an impartial inquiry. Too many government agencies covering their asses.

If they ever do figure it out, it'll all get translated into technical gibberish to keep us away and to make lawsuits difficult. Oh sure, two years down the line some Panel might make some recommendations that will prevent the same kind of accident from recurring, but the recs will get buried in red tape. And anyway, the follow-up on disasters is never as good as the event itself.

Don't worry about the details of why it happened. Take it from me—it happened. I was up there, and I shot some film

---

ways in which the Khmer Rouge carried out their revolution was precisely *pativattana*. They attempted to obliterate all that was not ancient Khmer.

Their first action, the evacuation of the cities, was a warning of what was to come. They might as well have designated Angkor Wat the capital and killed the entire urban population there and then. They might have done just that had the leaders not recognized the administrative difficulties involved—or had the cadres not wanted to take their revenge on those who hadn't completely shared their experience of having the fabric of their lives ripped apart by American bombs.

The Khmer Rouge made no attempt to re-educate the urban population or to alter their consciousness. A stain was a stain. It could only

of it. We got a call about it no more than fifteen minutes after the wreck. The report was that there'd been one hell of an explosion on impact, and that there was diesel and sulphur and wheat all mixed together and burning. They said as many as thirty were dead, but they didn't have an exact count. Anything more than ten dead is a major story, and we were told to fly in there from Vancouver to get film and commentary for Pacific Region news.

Hinton is the small town near the site of the wreck. It's not much to look at—Hinton, I mean—a nowhere town in the middle of nowhere. God knows why anybody would want to live there. The place stinks from the pulp mill on the other side of the highway. Maybe that was why the sulphur cars were on the freight, who knows? We didn't ask. Those are the kinds of 'whys' television journalism isn't geared to.

Hinton is so goddamned small we had to charter a plane to get in there. There are no scheduled flights, and even if there had been, booking in would have been a joke, because reporters and camera crews were flying in from all over the country. There were piles of guys I'd worked with before, and if you could've forgotten about the snow and stink and the pigpen conditions, you could have taken the Hinton hospital lobby for a newsmen's convention. That was an illusion that passed quickly. Hinton is the kind of place that does its level best to remind you where you are.

As for the train wreck, I've never seen such a fucking mess.

---

be obliterated, exterminated. Within months of the take-over, the civil servants, police, and soldiers of the old regime were killed or condemned to death in absentia. All the Chinese, Vietnamese, Cham and Islamic peoples within the Khmer zone were declared traitors and either executed or marked for execution. Some escaped into Vietnam and Thailand. Most did not.

Those who survived the evacuation were placed in rural agricultural communes, where they were forced to work as virtual slaves on vast and often pointless communal projects: earth-filled dams that soon collapsed; irrigation projects that simply flooded previously viable farmland. In these communes, the stated purpose of which was to stave off famine by rebuilding the country's agricultural capacity, each

Or smelled one. Most of the diesel went up on impact, so no one got any footage of the initial fireball. I heard from one or two local yokels that it was pretty spectacular. There was enough diesel blown across the wrecked cars that it ignited the sulphur and wheat, and by the time we arrived the sulphur was cooking steak and kidney pie in the wreckage. From what I can figure at least one wheat car broke apart directly on top of the passenger coaches so that the wheat sifted down inside. Well, you get the idea. Poor fuckers. Most of the victims got trapped in the wreckage and were either suffocated or fried.

Only the front two day-coaches got completely crunched. Most of the people on the rear of the train were okay. The railroad puts the sleeper cars on the back end of the train, and those people just got banged around a little. Dunno why they put the sleeper cars on the back. The day coaches are always more crowded, and if they'd had a sleeper or two in close it's a sure thing fewer people would have died.

They had the surviving passengers in the small local hospital when we got there, about eighty of them in all. The medical teams had arrived just before we did, and they were trying to sort out the cuts and bruises from the more serious injuries. We did some interviews with the ones who were standing around in the hospital lobby waiting to be processed through and bussed into Edmonton. They didn't have much to say beyond "Wow!" Not surprising, since most of them were asleep when it happened.

---

citizen was required to construct and submit a verbal autobiography to the commune and its Khmer Rouge cadres. The autobiographies were not used, as might be expected, to create a sense of community. Instead, they were used to identify traitors. Those who revealed that they had been doctors, technicians, Buddhist monks, teachers, intellectuals or students were executed. Having studied abroad, speaking French or English or any of the Vietnamese dialects, having a fair skin or wearing glasses were likewise cause for capital punishment.

Education was administered to the young, but it consisted solely of political indoctrination. Children who erred in reciting the catechism of the new brand of truth were summarily killed in the classroom, beaten to death by their classmates or strangled by the instructor, who

The police and the railroad officials weren't great material, either. Both had obviously gotten instructions from their headquarters, so all they'd tell us was either "we won't know for a day or two" or "no comment". Dullsville. One of the Toronto reporters teased a dumb police corporal into making some remarks, but they weren't choice ones, just stupid. They were interesting enough to get aired, and probably ugly enough to get the poor clown sent to the North Pole.

There weren't any bodies. At least there weren't any that they were willing to show us. After a few hours someone found out that the officials didn't have the slightest idea how many had been killed, because they didn't know how many had been on the train in the first place. Computer malfunction or something. That meant they didn't know exactly how many victims were still in the wreck. And the wreck was still smouldering and would continue to, they said, for maybe a couple of days. That was okay, but smouldering wrecks aren't exactly dramatic.

I rented a chopper and we overflew the site. Got some good footage out of that. After that we hung around rescue headquarters down at the train station for another three or four hours and shot film of whatever local idiot would talk to us. There wasn't much action. About 4:00 p.m. I put everything I'd shot on the charter plane and sent it back to Vancouver. Then I phoned my Bureau Chief in Vancouver and gave him a situation report.

"Pick up what you can," he said, "and hang tough."

---

was usually a Khmer Rouge not much older than the children.

The logic of the Khmer Rouge atrocities is so simple I have to repeat it to avoid any mistakes about what it was. They were rooting out and exterminating all that was not purely and indigenously ignorant of modern urban civilization. If a person could perform any task that was not done in the twelfth century reign of Suryavram II, that person was a traitor. A Khmer Rouge slogan says it all:

Preserve them—no profit
Exterminate them—no loss
We will burn the old grass and the new will grow.

I asked him how long he wanted us there, and after a second he said he wanted some decent victim footage. "Wait till they bring a body out of the wreck. I want that on film."

Apparently every other crew had been given roughly the same instruction. I wasn't exactly knocked dead because it meant we'd have to stay overnight. Worse, the Rescue Chief claimed that it might not be possible to bring out any bodies right away, even though they were sure no one in there was still alive. The sulphur and wheat mix was volatile, they said, and they didn't want to take a bulldozer to the buried coach because they didn't want to risk a flareup. When someone suggested they should have a better reason than just that, they said that they didn't want to mangle the corpses more than they already were. Humanitarian considerations. What a load of crap.

So that was a drag. Most of us went down to the local hotel. The Network Chief told us to leave a skeleton crew on line for the night in case anything good came up. I wasn't on it, thank Christ, so I had a couple of beers, watched the news, which was out of Atlanta because the hotel had a dish. I finally got the local station on the screen, but that was hooked into Edmonton and only had their footage.

By morning, Network had edited all the stuff they had into a package. I thought I caught some of my footage in a couple of places. It was hard to tell, since all the crews were shooting the same things. They did run one interview I was sure we did, so I got a little bit of the big action.

This slogan, interestingly, shows precisely the same limited logic of ancient Khmer cut-and-burn agriculture. It serves until the natural vitality of the soil is exhausted. After that, the jungle returns, or the desert enters.

In three years and nine months of this "cleansing", as many as two million human beings died from executions, or from starvation and exhaustion. And in the famine that resulted from the collapse of the regime and the invasion by the Vietnamese, another 700,000 lives may have been lost.

■

At breakfast I talked with the night crew, which'd just come back from the location. They'd got nothing. But word had slipped out that they might have something for us soon, so we finished breakfast and hustled our asses back out to the wreck. When we got here, the bastards still wouldn't give us anything solid. They kept referring us to the Rescue Chief, and he wasn't telling us anything either. Finally, someone cornered him just before lunch and got him to say they were bringing some victims out of the wreck around 2:00 p.m.

It was more like 3:00 p.m. before an ambulance appeared, and by that time most of the crews were completely pissed off and irritable. I sure as hell was. It was colder than a nun's underwear and it'd begun to snow a little, and all of us were freezing our butts off standing around waiting. I wasn't dressed for a blizzard, and neither was anyone else except the Edmonton guys.

So when three guys pulled up in an ambulance, we damned near cheered. They told us we could set up, and about six of them, including the Rescue Chief, walked single file down into the wreckage like a church procession and disappeared. They came back after thirty minutes or so, carrying a single body bag.

We shot the entire event from start to finish. There wasn't much to it, actually. They wouldn't let us get in too close, and the body bag was closed anyway. There was no way we could talk them into opening it up. After that was finished, most of us packed it up and left the crew from Edmonton to do mop

---

Like the Congo, Cambodia has produced particular figures and images of horror. For us, these involve the Khmer Rouge's abandonment of Western technologies, and the several exceptions they made. It is these exceptions and the ways in which they were employed that provide the clearest images of Khmer Rouge barbarism.

One of the retained technologies was radio. Its continued use may have something to do with the fact that Pol Pot studied radio journalism in Paris during his stay there in the 1950s. But more probably, radio was retained because it requires no written language, and provides neither documentation that can be studied nor specific images. Like television, radio serves up and supports illiteracy. At the same time, it lends itself to centralized dissemination of informa-

up. We were in the air forty-five minutes later, and I got home in time to watch the news. The new film didn't make it, but I watched it at eleven. It was okay, I guess. Nothing spectacular.

The shit hit the fan the next day. Someone found out that the bastards had been putting us on. There'd been no body in the bag. They weren't ready to get any bodies out of the wreck for another two days, but they wanted to get us out of there. So they took a body bag down to the site, filled it with debris and let us film it. Can you imagine that? A bunch of flatfoots and hicks putting us on like that?

They could have filled the body bag with bananas for all I cared. I mean, we bought the hoax, and if we did the public sure wasn't going to see through it. It looked real. So sure, we wanted out of there just as bad as they wanted us out. I mean, who the hell wants to sit in a snowbank in the middle of nowhere freezing your ass off. But if you're going to pull a stunt, you'd better take it all the way. You don't do what they did. They emptied the body bag in plain sight of somebody from the Edmonton crew a couple of hours after we left.

The Bureau Chief was really pissed off, as you can imagine. He and a bunch of other brass flew up there with a crew and held a kangaroo court, calling the railroad people and the cops everything in the book and laying down the law about the sanctity of the media and what could happen if government employees started staging events like that. And of course they filmed it. It got a seven minute lead story on the National.

---

tion. In the communes, radio propaganda broadcasts during meals were part and parcel of the regimen of forced labour and executions: the disembodied voice from the speaker exhorting *pativattana*—the return to the past.

Also retained was the use of still photography. It was used for a limited and very revealing purpose. Traitors to the Communist Party (which was called *Angka*—the Organization) received more elaborate and brutal treatment than did those who were merely unsuitable for the *pativattana*. Unsuitable citizens—"New People" they were called—were marked for "simple" extermination, and were put to death in the most efficient way at hand. They were stabbed, strangled or clubbed to death, and their bodies dumped in convenient and

Network loved it, I guess.

But I guess if you're sitting in the executive suite, you get to believe that the news is supposed to be authentic. I don't claim to understand how Network executives think. I just shoot whatever I'm told to shoot. If there's a body in the bag, well, that's great. But it's the bag people wanted to see, and I don't think they really care who or what is inside it, just so long as they can believe it's the real thing, live and in colour.

---

usually public locations. Bomb craters were a favourite. The "New People" were regarded as weeds, and were treated accordingly; rooted out and disposed of as quickly and efficiently as possible. No one photographs weeds.

Traitors to *Angka* were regarded as a serious disease. Party officials and functionaries accused of traitorous tendencies were brought, along with their families, to S21 (or Tuol Sleng), a Phnom Penh high school converted into a prison/interrogation centre. Incoming inmates were photographed on arrival. After that, between sessions of torture, they were compelled to write elaborate confessions in which they enumerated their crimes, always concluding with usually absurd confessions of life-long allegiance to the American CIA, the Russian KGB,

Outside the Diamond

People who follow professional baseball can tell you Reggie Jackson is an attractive ballplayer. I will, and without a single reservation. I like the way he stands in at the plate to bat, flat-footed and ponderous. I like the way he swings and misses—something he has done more often than anyone since the game's statistics began to be recorded. I particularly like the way he slams his bat down and watches the ball when he knows he's hit one out. I enjoy watching him run the bases, even now that he's forty and is slowing down. And one of the purest joys I've known is watching this great ballplayer catch fly balls with his forehead or kneecaps. I even like the way he spits sunflower seeds from between his front teeth, although that's more curiosity than admiration. I can't quite figure out how he does it.

I'm a couple of years older than Jackson, but he's one of my heroes anyway. I've modelled parts of my own game on his, even though I'm white, slow afoot, and at best a mediocre sandlot catcher. I chose him as a model partly because we both

---

or to the Vietnamese. More often than not, victims confessed allegiance to all three. The confessions were carefully transcribed and filed away with the snapshots, just as in any efficient bureaucracy. Then the victims were put to death. Only seven of Tuol Sleng's 20,000 inmates survived *Angka*'s zealous program of self-cleansing.

When the invading Vietnamese armies entered Phnom Penh in 1979, they captured Tuol Sleng and its archive in a relatively intact state. They have since turned the buildings into a museum, presenting it as a Nazi-style concentration camp. The choicest among the snapshots found in the archive now decorate the walls of the museum. Along with the instruments of torture and death, these snapshots now overlook the same rooms in which the human beings they depict were

hit left-handed, and partly because I have an almost mystical aversion to playing in the outfield, where I catch flies less successfully than he does. As a matter of record, one summer a few years back I matched him home run for home run, and I got up to twenty-eight before my team decided they couldn't take it anymore. They found a place to play with a right field fence quite a lot farther away from home plate than the 150 feet I'd grown accustomed to. Damn them. I finished the season with thirty homers, nine short of the number he hit.

That's where the similarity between Reggie Jackson and I ends. For me, baseball is only recreation. When I take my ego and my modest skills onto the field, there are no spectators, no television cameras, no million dollar professional salaries to justify. My essential existence is radically different from Jackson's, which is professional and public, a nexus of public observation.

Unlike Jackson, I am an obscure witness to what occurs in history and in time and space. I have, for instance, witnessed a distinction between history and baseball. They are *not* one and the same. Baseball is ritual and geometry, a zone of arbitrary and often sentimental relationships where time is reorganized into discrete episodes called innings, and where space is rational and free of external threat. An Angel or a Yankee can exist in the same field. In baseball, a player—a Reggie Jackson—may win or lose, but the game goes on, there is a game tomorrow, next week, there will be games next year. History, to put it

---

tortured and executed.

Tuol Sleng reveals a number of seemingly bizarre ironies. One of them is that Western technologies conditioned and at times enabled the most brutal Khmer Rouge practices. Another is that the technologies the Khmer Rouge retained are curiously typical of modern post-industrial civilization's preoccupation with disposable commodities, and with the kind of cybernetic and administrative efficiencies that lead to generic information and commodities.

The Tuol Sleng torture manual, which was found among the captured torture instruments, snapshots and documents, indicates, along with the grotesque record-keeping, that the use of torture was aimed not to punish error or even to wipe out evil, but as a means of deduc-

briefly and bluntly, no longer has any of those comforting properties.

Outside the diamond, I've found Reggie Jackson to be rather less attractive. As a matter of record, there are quite a number of things about him I dislike intensely. I dislike the way he dresses. I dislike the way he talks and I dislike the way he thinks about himself. Part of my dislike relates to a long-standing distaste I have for an organization of brainoids called the Mensa Club. Jackson is a proud member of Mensa, and he yaks constantly, tastelessly and often remarkably stupidly about his 160 I.Q.

Let me put all this dislike into a single item. I dislike Reggie Jackson for his habit of referring to himself in the third person. If you follow baseball at all, you've heard his pronouncements: Reggie Jackson is still an everyday player, Reggie Jackson really can catch fly balls, Reggie Jackson doesn't like it when the press gets on him too much. Once I heard him go a step beyond that, referring to himself as a generic substance: *A Reggie Jackson can't go out and hit home runs every day.* Outside the diamond a Reggie Jackson appears to be a smart-talking asshole in a pimp suit; a generic substance I can do without.

But a while back I caught a two-inch item on the sports page of my local newspaper that has altered my opinion of an off-the-diamond Reggie Jackson. Maybe, just maybe, Jackson knows something that makes him speak of himself as an object. And maybe, just maybe, he knows what kind of a world we're

---

ing, clarifying and creating unanimous generic information. In the eye of *Angka*, all inmates were the same. Their confessions were made to show identical foreign allegiances, their impurities were always foreign in origin. The Khmer Rouge not only killed these people, they destroyed all differentiation and identity among them before they did so.

The photographing of victims reveals the compulsive nature of this preoccupation. Photography is immediate and ostensibly unmediated. The development process in photography consists of the interaction of invisible chemicals and light on the surface of a blank piece of paper. The record-keeping at Tuol Sleng added a macabre dimension to the photographic process. Each image that appeared on the blank sur-

living in better than almost anyone.

So you can see what I mean, let me dilate that two-inch newspaper anecdote into a story—a dramatized eye-witness account. To do this, I'll have to invade the privacy of Jackson's mind. Not polite, but as a writer of fiction, it's my professional right. Jackson can stand the inconvenience one more time. After all, he does get to play baseball all summer.

●

It is spring training, and Jackson's team, the California Angels, are headquartered in Phoenix, Arizona. One of the reasons they're there, I suspect, is because the team owner, former singing cowboy hero Gene Autry, owns a resort hotel in Phoenix. He may even own the rest of Phoenix, I don't know.

When we pick him up, Reggie Jackson is walking through the parking lot of the hotel, dressed in his pimp suit, his gold chains, and his expensive watch: easily recognizable. I'm not sure what's going on in the privacy of his 160 I.Q. mind, although it's a safe bet to assume that he's hungry because he's headed for the hotel's restaurant. For all I know, he's thinking about his biorhythms or his latest astrology chart, or he's reciting last year's American League ERA's and the repertoires of the pitchers he will face in the coming year. Notwithstanding this characteristic exercise of his I.Q., his arms hang down, aggressively and slightly off-balance, in an equally characteristic way.

---

face was automatically that of an already condemned traitor. Yet the Khmer Rouge felt compelled to confirm the traitors' images at the same time as they were utterly denying their individual identity. I catch myself wondering what happened to those who were photographed with defective cameras or with defective film. Were their lives spared because the image did not appear?

Yet another icon of Western technology the Khmer Rouge used was the disposable plastic bag. These bags were presumably much the same as the ones we use in our supermarkets to purchase potatoes, apples and other perishables. The Khmer Rouge used them for executions. The bags were pulled over the heads of victims, tightened around their necks, and held there until the victim suffocated. The bodies were

Even while he's walking across a parking lot to a restaurant, he looks as if he's approaching the plate to bat: intimidating.

As he strides toward the restaurant's entrance, two men in an aging Buick spot him. They quickly circle the parking lot, rubber squealing, to intercept him. The driver cranks down his window as the car pulls up beside Jackson.

"Hey motherfucker!" he shouts.

Jackson stops in his tracks, a weary expression on his face, and stares neutrally at the man. He's been here before. Either it is some white punks harassing what they assume is a wealthy middle-class black man, or it is hostile fans, who, having recognized him, want to score some private brownie points. Later, they will tell their friends how they sassed a Reggie Jackson and got away with it.

Jackson decides that his assailant is from the former category. The punk is an aging California-style hippie, thin, squizzle-haired and dirty, and quite probably whacked out of his skull on drugs. He watches as the punk pulls the lumbering Buick over to the curb and leaps out. From the other side of the car comes another punk, this one bigger, heavier, and just as filthy and ill-kempt. But judging from his body english, this one isn't quite so eager for a confrontation.

The skinny punk stumbles across the tarmac toward Jackson, his thumbs hooked in his belt loops. Jackson takes a quick inventory. The jeans the punk wears are splattered with food and auto grease, but they're new: no hippie patches. The guy

---

then disposed of—dumped into ditches and bomb craters with the plastic bags still tied around their necks.

The painting-over of the signs in Phnom Penh carries another set of messages. Remember that all the signs—traffic signs, advertising, location and identity markers of every kind—were obliterated. They were painted over, but because they were not removed, they were transformed into transmitters of non-information. For us, those blank signs should serve as a bleak warning about the depth to which the Khmer Rouge penetrated the nature of the world we are in. On the surface, the blanked signs are symbolic of the Khmer Rouge's contempt for the capacity of human imagination and memory and their belief that all human beings are *tabula rasa*. But there is more to it.

probably drinks beer and smokes grass, but that's all. He isn't wired. There are tattoos on both his forearms. That tells Jackson the man has done time, probably some medium security rap—the tattoos aren't very large or elaborate and there are none on the backs of his hands. Jackson squares his shoulders warily, looking for a concealed weapon.

"Hey, man, I *know* you," the punk announces.

"You don't know nothing, assholes," Jackson answers coldly.

"No, no!" the punk shouts, growing more excited. "I know who you *are!*"

"Big fucking deal," Jackson replies without altering his tone. "So do I. But that isn't going to change anything for either of us."

The second punk has shuffled up behind his companion and is staring at Jackson with a mixture of awe and curiosity. A neutral, Jackson decides, unless the other one tries something.

As if cued by Jackson's thought, the "something" materializes in the hand of the first punk: a switchblade. It's a good one, spring-loaded, the slender blade about four inches long. The punk swishes it back and forth in the air between himself and Jackson as if the blade were a paintbrush and he were painting a masterpiece. Then he moves a step closer. Jackson holds his ground. Wouldn't be intelligent to show fear. Not here, not now.

"Gimme your fucking wallet," the punk says, narrowing his eyes in an attempt to intimidate.

One of the valid criticisms of all Marxist-Leninist governments is that they act out of essentially the same belief. Yet the particular symbols of Khmer Rouge barbarism seem to derive more from the West than from the Marxist-Leninist world. Each painted-over sign in Phnom Penh, each Tuol Sleng archival snapshot reveals a secret and unacknowledged collusion with precisely those tendencies of the Western world they sought to wipe out: the medium without any message, or the technical process that undermines or destroys the identity of those it is intended to benefit.

6

In the face of Cambodia, and in what appear to be the last darkening

Jackson stares at him for moment, and then slowly removes his alligator skin wallet from his back pocket. Without taking his eyes off the punk, he places it on the pavement at his feet. Then he removes his wrist-watch and puts that on top of the wallet. Then the gold chain from his other wrist.

"Come here and take them, asshole," he says. "There's four thousand dollars in the wallet, and the watch is worth three thousand. The chain's 22 carat gold. You and your pal could buy a six-month supply of sniffing glue with this stuff."

"Hand them to me," the punk answers, suddenly sounding less aggressive. "Pick them up and bring them to me."

Jackson says nothing. He shrugs his shoulders, shifts his hips slightly and rubs his knuckles. The message is an eloquent one. The knife doesn't scare him, and he has outsmarted the punk. The moment the punk goes for the loot, he, Reggie Jackson, is going to kick his empty head off his puny neck. The heavy-set punk puts his hand on his friend's shoulder, but the skinny punk shrugs it off.

"No!" he shouts, more to Jackson than to his comrade. "I *want* this black motherfucker!"

"I'm waiting," Jackson says. "Make my day."

By now, some people in the parking lot are aware of the confrontation. None of them comes close enough to interfere—trouble is trouble, and no one here wants to be an official witness. They're interested, but only abstractly, like it's the news on television; a celebrity event in the making, the kind

---

days of literate culture, I feel compelled to identify those contemporary writers with whom I am aligned. At first I am surprised by those I select. None are writers from the mainstream of English-speaking culture. Most come, as I do, from distant outposts of progress, and all are exiles of one sort or another. There is another surprise. Most of them write in the English language. A first list includes V.S. Naipaul, Alexander Trocchi, Breyten Breytenbach, Nadine Gordimer, John Berger. A second list includes Salman Rushdie, Günter Grass, Miroslav Milosz, Jacobo Timerman, Primo Levi. They are not the writers I respected and tried to emulate in my student days, and none of them are Americans. More surprising yet, none of them are from my own country. Then I see the logic of it.

they see on their sets every day. Perhaps they believe that somewhere, invisible to them, the omniscient cameras are rolling. So they stay near their cars, frozen, keeping their distance, even those who are baseball fans and know Reggie Jackson is involved. If it goes big, they can watch it later on, at home or in their hotel rooms, where it will be more secure and real to them.

Jackson remains perfectly relaxed, perfectly still. But to the punks he seems to be growing larger by the second. He is Reggie Jackson after all, the smartest, toughest, proudest black man in baseball. And Jackson knows that it shows.

The skinny punk's resolve crumbles first, and he steps back. The other punk doesn't move. He is gazing at the wallet longingly. For a moment Jackson wonders if the big punk might be the real problem; he may yet go for it. He tenses himself. Then the second punk steps back too, and the two punks turn together and run to the Buick.

The car doesn't start, and Jackson chuckles as he watches the skinny punk fumbling with the ignition, trying to get the erratic starter to co-operate. The motor kicks into life, the punk revs it to a scream and punches the automatic transmission into gear at the crescendo. The old car lurches through the parking lot trailing smoke and burned tire rubber, jumps a dividing island and disappears down the road. Jackson picks up his wallet, watch and chain, chuckles to himself and heads into the restaurant. Breakfast. People keep their distance as he

---

When I was at university I was chasing after what I believed were the writers of a high civilization that was my own by right of birth and access, but temporarily incomprehensibly alien because of my lack of sophistication. I studied and emulated Ezra Pound, Charles Olson, and the writers of the New American Poetry. Almost all of them were poets, and most were equally obsessed with breaking down a kind of democratic authority they found personally stultifying and repressive, and with reifying that same authority as a means of liberating the general population from ignorance and preventing the spread of totalitarianism.

Behind that small, self-contradicting group was a parade of writers from the past, most of whom provided ideological and textual support

approaches the entrance. He is Reggie Jackson, an extremely large and intelligent man, fresh from danger, and you'd better believe it.

•

The restaurant hostess, an attractive sloe-eyed blonde, knows who Jackson is. She's also aware that he's just encountered some trouble in the parking lot. She seats him at a window table that looks away from the entrance. Jackson refuses the seating but not the table, and takes a chair that faces the entrance, sighing as he sits down. He's not frightened by the parking lot encounter, just annoyed. Sometimes it's goddamn tiring being a Reggie Jackson.

"I hope there wasn't real trouble, Mr. Jackson," the hostess says with her most winning smile. "Coffee?"

"Please," replies Jackson, then adds, "the trouble was real enough, but we managed to work our way through it."

"We?" asks the hostess.

"Me," Jackson answers curtly. "A figure of speech."

"Oh," says the hostess, her sunny smile breaking up a little. "I hope you're okay."

Jackson glances at the menu, orders breakfast, and settles in to speed-read the newspaper the hostess brings him. Several other Angels players come in—younger guys. They don't sit with him.

---

for their world view. Further afield was the traditional survey of world literature promulgated by modern English departments—Spenser, Milton, the English Romantics, nineteenth-century English novelists, and moderns like Lawrence, Hemingway, Joyce, Eliot, and Gertrude Stein.

I didn't read writers from my own country until it became clear to me that I really was going to be a writer and not an academic scholar or literary historian. I've since discovered some very good writers here, but I resist placing any of them on my list. I have to think that one through carefully, and the reason I come up with doesn't please me.

In the culture I am part of, there is a great deal of encouragement for apolitically experimental writing, which is to say, for writers to

Oh, they like him okay. But they know that Jackson's a private man outside the ballpark, and they know he expects his professional associates to respect his privacy. Everybody else is after it and after him—the press and the media, guys writing stupid stories and articles about what he thinks and feels. They can't know what goes on in Reggie Jackson's mind. And they don't really care, either. Then there are the thieves who strip his Mercedes during games, women trying to pick him up whenever he goes into a restaurant or a bar, disgruntled fans harassing him as he leaves the ballpark after a team loss. It goes on and on. Those punks are just an episode. One of many, and not a very interesting one. As incidents in the life of Reggie Jackson go, no big deal, no great effort expended.

•

Except, apparently, it isn't over yet. As Jackson looks up, the Buick is pulling up outside the restaurant, double parking in front of the entrance. The skinny punk leaps out and charges inside. He scans the room until he spots Jackson.

"Hey!" he hollers, pointing his finger at Jackson. "Hey you! I need to talk to you!"

What now? Jackson thinks. He considers ignoring the punk, but then makes several swift calculations: this is, after all, Gene Autry's restaurant. If there's got to be a brawl let's make sure it's not inside where people can get hurt, property damaged.

---

elaborate upon already existing forms. But there is no impetus for writers here to use their craft in order to learn, or to effect political and social change, and writers are subtly discouraged from confronting ultimate questions. Hence, I can't find what I need to know from my own compatriots. Nothing, at least, about a world that has Cambodia in it.

I have essentially the same criticism of my compatriots as I have of the modern writers presented to me by the English department. With one or two exceptions, the exercise of their skills is too formal and their subject matter too narrow. Consequently their work seems either infraculturally self-occupied, or purely psychological in its consequences. For almost all of them, heritage culture and personality

The hostess comes over to Jackson's table and stands next to him. She appears disturbed. "Mr. Jackson?" she pleads, as if to signify to him that it isn't her fault.

Jackson puts his hands on her shoulders and turns her firmly aside. "This gentleman is my problem. You just keep people back, if you can. I can deal with this in one minute."

He walks heavily toward the punk. In his mind, he's striding toward home plate, concentrating, consciously sending off waves of incredibly aggressive mental energy. Jackson notes that the punk hasn't pulled his blade, so he moves close enough to him that he can coldcock him if he tries to bring the blade out.

"You assaulted me in the parking lot," the punk says, loudly. Very loudly, so that everyone in the restaurant can hear it.

Jackson laughs, also loudly. "If I assaulted you, you'd be in hospital right now, punko. Now why don't you give everyone here a break and clear out of here before you really do get hurt. I've had about as much of this as I need."

Jackson and the punk recognize the error at the same time.

"Hit me," the punk says, excitedly. "Go ahead." He steps in closer and thrusts forward his jaw. "Do it. I got lawyers. Hit me. Come on."

Jackson recoils ever so slightly as he recognizes the small danger he's in. If he hits the punk in front of all these people he will get sued. For a bundle. And the punk will probably win the case, too. Reggie Jackson can't go around slugging every half-baked nitwit who challenges him. Better to give him the

---

are subject matter enough. They think of their work as contributing to heritage culture; their lack of cultural effectiveness and influence made up for by economic security provided by jobs in the universities or by modest government grants. Many of them are resourceful and intelligent people, but they interest me more because of what they *might* write than for what they have written. I might get to talk to them someday, and we might influence one another to do something different. Meanwhile, there are other writers in the world who are more clearly engaged in a contemporary discourse.

A few years ago my university-gathered education began to slip away—as it has for most people with literature degrees—like water off a duck's back. I found that I was going back to those writers who'd

wallet and the wristwatch.

"You *want* this wallet?" he says, removing it from his back pocket and extending it to the punk. "You want it, you got it."

The punk steps closer still, still offering his jaw. "Come on motherfucker. Punch me out. That's what you want to do, ain't it."

Jackson laughs. "Tempting," he says. "But you're confusing me with someone else. I'm Reggie Jackson, not Billy Martin."

His grin widens for just a split second as he experiences his own witticism. Then, unaccountably, the grin is replaced by a frown. Before Jackson can decide whose witticism it is, and exactly how witty it was, a police officer appears and grabs the punk from behind, pinioning his arms. Behind the police officer is a man with a camera. The press is here, naturally. Usually they arrive first.

For a moment, right in the midst of the tumble of events, Jackson's identity is reaffirmed for himself. The eye of the world. Mr. October. Mr. Controversy. Thank god he has his 160 I.Q. to protect him.

"This gentleman seems to want something," Jackson tells the police officer. "First he asked me for my wallet, and now he wants me to punch him so he can sue me. So far, he's come up dry."

The police officer gives the punk a not-so-gentle shake. "Okay, buster," he says. "Let's get you out of this establishment and

---

influenced me while I was still a naive colonial ransacking the small public library of my home town for books by writers like Dostoevsky, Sartre, Pasternak, Thomas Malory. Added to the list were a number of Greek and Roman writers picked up along the way, along with poets like Rilke and Mayakovsky.

I realize that this is an idiosyncratic list. My readings of these writers is probably even more idiosyncratic, but I can explain it relatively easily by means of a single paradigm. This paradigm is lodged in the poetry of Samuel Taylor Coleridge, and it is this: I can no longer read "The Rime of the Ancient Mariner" or *Kubla Khan*, works of "visionary" imagination. I can, however, read his "Fears in Solitude" rather easily, because he wrote it as an attempt to see into the political and

check you and your friend out there for warrants."

He turns the punk around forcibly and glances over his shoulder at Jackson. "Sorry about this, Mr. Jackson," he says. "Have a fine season now, y'hear?"

Jackson smiles at the departing police officer. Nice. Have a fine season. Even in his own mind, he's aware that having a fine season isn't going to be as easy as getting rid of these stupid punks has been. It's getting tougher and tougher every year to play baseball. He's nearing forty, and even though he's the only man in history with an I.Q. of 160 to hit more than five hundred home runs, it's getting harder to coerce his body into co-operating with the daily grind of baseball. Mentally he's prepared, of course, but there are more and more days when that isn't quite enough.

Jackson returns to his table and settles in for his breakfast. The police cruiser remains outside with the two punks in the back seat, the blue and red lights spinning in the hazy morning sun. Then another cruiser appears, and the punks, in handcuffs now, are transferred to it. The second cruiser pulls away. A tow truck pulls up seconds later, hooks up the old Buick and takes that away. Then the original cruiser drives away. The departing police officer waves at Jackson as he passes the restaurant window.

•

---

social imagination of his time. The poem, though considerably less successful aesthetically than the more famous ones, carries a quite different kind of content. It is, in the deepest sense, prophesy. It is prophesy that I am after, not visions of high imagination. I want to see how and where and why we're impaled on the spike of the present dilemma.

•

My rereading of literature has been conditioned by something more than simply having grown up. In the past few years I've become convinced that the world has undergone a fundamental change. After April 29th, 1975, with the military defeat and withdrawal of the United

Reggie Jackson finishes breakfast, absorbed in his thoughts. What is he thinking? Perhaps he is thinking about the diamond, and the zone of danger and desire that surrounds its symmetries. For him, that zone is filled with others, their desires, fantasies, their attempts—sweet or belligerent—to attach themselves to him. A zone where he must defend himself constantly against those desires and fantasies.

The sloe-eyed blond hostess removes the dishes and refills his coffee cup, leaning in front of him so he can see the firm young breasts nestled in their B cups. As she does it, she apologizes once again for the unpleasantness. Jackson ignores her, but does note the odd, slow way she pronounces his name: *Mist-er Jackt-son*, putting that extra 't' into it like she's making him up as she says it, all for herself. She doesn't want an autographed baseball like the police officer probably wanted for his kids, but she wants something else. When you're a Reggie Jackson, everybody wants something.

His mind drifts back to the punks. They'll be back. If not for him, then for someone else like him. Bob Boone, the catcher, maybe. Another intelligent man, Jackson thinks, mentally reviewing Boone's seasonal and lifetime stats. Not quite so intelligent as a Reggie Jackson, and nowhere near the hitter. Handles pitchers well. Fair strike zone judgement. How would he have made out with those punks? Jackson plays out this theoretical drama in his mind. At a certain point in the action he has to interfere in order to save Boone from injury. He catches

---

States from Southeast Asia, Western Civilization began, almost involuntarily, a process of transformation that seems intent on effecting the disappearance of ideology and of nationalism—of nationhood itself. Ideology and nationalism were the ideas that the modern Imperium built itself with. But ideology and nationalism were also the chief intellectual weapons used to push America out of Vietnam and Cambodia. They were as impossible to defeat in the hands of the insurgents as they were in the hands of those who first made use of them.

Since then, the redefinition and global circulation of the West's overpoweringly vital political and economic ideas has led to a peculiar brew of indigenous religion, local culture, and Marxism in a planet overcrowded with peoples hungry for material comforts. Nationalism and

himself doing it, and stops, midway through.

Or maybe I do it. Sticking Bob Boone into this story is just an irrelevant intrusion, Jackson and I think at the same moment. The necessary recognition factor isn't there with Boone, Jackson interrupts. To those punks he'd only be another white man in a parking lot. But I wonder: *How real were you to those mangy punks this morning, Reggie Jackson?*

Jackson's head snaps up, and he looks out the window. Nothing there. No one. An absurd thought rattles through Jackson's brain, one that he rejects instantly, then recalls. He turns it over and over, like an alien egg that hatches, rebuilds its shell, then begins to hatch again. There's something else going on here, Reggie Jackson thinks to himself. Maybe this is not happening to me. Maybe, somewhere far away, someone else is making all this up, and I am not thinking what I am thinking at all.

He puts the thought away. The Angels are playing the Astros this afternoon.

That's real, he thinks.

---

ideology have become the weapons of the weak.

And so the Imperium of Western Civilization has begun to reformulate itself by dematerializing, *by becoming form*—artificially accelerating the process that began after the Second World War. Long before Marshall McLuhan pinpointed it with a catchy name, the arguments over the primacy and relationship between form and content, medium and message was raging in every quarter of Western Civilization. Indeed, one could argue that it began with the Gutenberg press, or with the Industrial Revolution, or with any advance in technology that enabled more efficient reproduction of objects and images.

It is still going on in every intellectual and applied technological discipline, now at fantastically accelerated velocities. In the process, the jungle Conrad saw being shelled has been reduced to a chaos of twisted roots and rubble. At the same time, the Third World shows an increasing reluctance to continue to be the unrewarded source of raw materials for the Imperium. As a result, the Imperium's material well-being has come increasingly to rest on its technological ability to generate and then merchandise attractively opaque forms and commodities: beads and trinkets to bemuse the natives. Everything changes. And it does not change at all.

Let it be recognized that the defeat of Western military technology has not, as was expected a decade ago by everyone sympathetic to the Left, resulted in universal social justice in the Third World. If

Lamps

The two German P.O.W.s were Asian, and seemed almost blissfully indifferent to the rough conditions of their incarceration. They spoke to one another in a language that Allied Intelligence Captain John Surry did not understand. In the absence of precise information he assumed that the language was that of a subregion of the Eastern Soviet Union. Probably, he decided, the two P.O.W.s were Russian peasants who had been captured by the Germans on the Eastern Front and induced to fight for Germany by the promise of adequate food and freedom from imprisonment. Such instances, he knew, were becoming common, although these were the first he'd encountered.

It was the aftermath of the Normandy Invasion and Captain Surry was an extremely busy man—busier than he had ever been in his life. Before the invasion, his work as an intelligence officer had consisted largely of tracking down rumours that only occasionally had substance: reports of a German agent outside Coventry that turned out to be a harmless old Home Guardsman

---

anything, more injustice, more exploitation, and more suffering exists now than in 1975, perhaps particularly in Southeast Asia. But at the same time, we should remember that the universal light the Imperial shelling of the jungle in 1890 promised has not appeared either. The Global Village renewed that promise, but it has not delivered. It has only made us all into impoverished natives.

That's why I've chosen my artistic companions from the interzone between the First and Third world, where an observer can still see the opaqueness of the Global Village, and can peer into and perhaps decipher that which is taking form in the dark oppressed villages, undistracted by the beads and trinkets that flood around us. Village and flood we understand, or should. Our understanding is the one defence

monitoring German radio transmissions, or a report of a small boat coming ashore near Hartlepool that proved to be a local fisherman coming in after twilight.

Captain Surry's current job was to interrogate incoming German prisoners for information on enemy military strengths and weaknesses. The schedule of interrogations went on for twelve hours a day, and in the pressure and routine of it, he processed his two strange prisoners and forgot about them. But before he forgot them, he did make a personal file on them which he placed in his desk drawer for more leisurely investigation.

About two weeks later, the two men came to his attention once more. They had become the focus of some unspecified trouble in the P.O.W. compound. Startlingly, the report on them stated that the two men had picked up a small but functional amount of English, and that they now showed no inclination to speak German. This, it seemed, was partly the source of the trouble. They were refusing to speak to their fellow captives.

He questioned the junior officer who had filed the report, and what he found out intrigued him still more. The officer said that the two men lived apart from the others—as far as was possible in the crowded camp. They had marked out a small territory near the margins of the fence, and except for taking their meals with the others, they stayed outdoors and inside their small patch of ground, squatting on their haunches and staring alternately at the barbed wire fences, the fields beyond, or at the sky—never into the camp itself. Surry recalled his own

---

we will have.

7

If experience was once a great teacher, it has ceased to be a teacher of political truths or social wisdoms. In the twentieth century it has taught people to be politically reactionary and socially fearful, and little more than that. The sole exception is now forty years old. The German death camps of World War II taught the Jews that they would have to become politically aggressive if they were to survive, either as individuals or as a culture. And that, and its political manifestation— Zionism—was educative. Now, even that lesson has been lost, or it

impressions of the two. There was something oddly exotic about the two men—an absence of the hostility and impatience that characterized most P.O.W.s. In these two, apparently, it was replaced by a cheerfulness that did not quite mask a very peculiar kind of resignation.

•

More than a month passed before Captain Surry had time to conduct another interrogation of the men. This time he passed over the routine intelligence-gathering questions about German troop disposition and the locations of strategic industries within enemy territory. Surry's motive was simple curiosity.

This interview was even shorter than the first. The P.O.W.s couldn't (or wouldn't) tell him anything about their origins, claiming to know no other place name than that of the camp itself. Indeed, they seemed to have only the barest recognition that the Allied forces holding them captive had ever been their enemies, or that Germany, in whose uniforms they were still clothed, was at war. They both carried German names, they neither admitted nor denied the authenticity of the names. Captain Surry was certain the names were false, but he could secure nothing else from them. During the interview he did get them to admit that they had reached the place they were in by train, although they could not say how long ago. After an hour of frustration, Captain Surry gave up, and wrote a recommendation

---

is being misread. What happened to Europe's Jews was unique only in that it happened to Europeans. Genocide is a common political pattern across the world, not a brutal injustice directed against one group.

Experience taught the survivors of Cambodia a kind of silence that is beyond fear. Perhaps they don't want the rest of the world infected, or perhaps they know that the infection is already pandemic. Cambodia is a visible manifestation of elements in human polity that appear to seek expression as relentlessly and resourcefully as the more kindly impulses to sing, to paint, to compose different textures of reality, and to articulate new and old ideas lucidly. Genocide, Violence, Cambodia and Art. In the face of them, I have to ask some questions—the hardest questions that present themselves.

that they be transported to England as refugee belligerents.

•

It was several more months before the two men were removed from the P.O.W camp and sent to finish the war in a camp in Southeast England. The move was ultimately made in the interests of their safety. There had been several ugly incidents arising out of their refusal to speak German, including a brutal beating at the hands of a still-militant group of Wehrmacht non-coms. It seemed that the two men had forgotten how to speak any German at all.

Their new quarters were just barely more palatable than the P.O.W. camp. The inmates at the new camp were mainly Eastern Europeans from outside the Axis alliance. Their countries had been within German control during the early stages of the war, but were now mostly in the hands of the Soviets.

Around the time the war was ending, a Russian interpreter was brought in to question the two men. He established only that they were not from any of the Soviet group of republics, and that they spoke none of the languages of the Soviet Union. Nor, he discovered, could he gain any information about them by questioning the other refugees. As before, the two men were politely solitary. They expressed no desire for anything the camp did not already provide. They spoke only when spoken to, and accepted their food, clothing and shelter from the weather with

---

The first question is the most obvious one: who am I to write about Cambodia from an armchair? I've never been within five thousand miles of Southeast Asia. How, almost two decades after the events began, can I usefully begin to pick at Cambodia as one who, having discovered a partly-healed but still pus-filled boil on his own body would? What can I say that will be meaningful? What can I know?

I have no defence against the accusation that I was ignorant about Cambodia for too long. I accuse myself, and I do not accept the ready excuses: that little information has been available, then or now; that I am not a citizen of any of the Imperial powers morally liable for the damages inflicted on Cambodia and its people. I am neither American, nor Vietnamese, Russian nor Chinese. And I am not Cam-

serene indifference, eschewing the comforts of the barracks whenever the elements permitted.

•

The war ended, and the wrangling over the carving-up of Europe began. As the summer passed into autumn, those in the refugee camps began their slow repatriation. It was slow because many countries had experienced changes in government that made many refugees reluctant to return. Several countries ceased to exist, while still other countries had been so devastated that their alienated citizens in the camps saw nothing to return to and sought to go elsewhere. Only the two men made no effort to leave the camp.

A year passed while the camps emptied. Some refugees went home, others emigrated. But the two mystery men stayed where they were, ignored because they demanded nothing, just as they had demanded nothing while the war was in progress. They complied with every demand made of them, obeyed every regulation and limitation with a cheerful neutrality, as if mere corporeal existence in the sanguine air of Southeastern England was entirely satisfactory to them.

While the world seemed to forget them, Captain Surry did not. For him, they had remained a puzzle, a welcome one from the patterns of grief, revenge and reparation that occupied him as the war ended and the exhausted world began the task of

---

bodian. I do not accept the excuse that the information that does exist has been suppressed in the most subtle of ways—by making it temporarily sensational and visible but conceptually and morally opaque.

The first excuse is unacceptable because in fact detailed information has been available for several years. The second excuse is unacceptable because I am a human being, and am therefore subject to, and capable of, the same brutalities as any human being. The third excuse is unacceptable because as an intellectual and an artist it is my job to understand and describe any profound threats that confront my species and planet.

Having said that, I feel compelled to point out that few of the analysts of Cambodia who have been in the country have been very

rebuilding civilization. After a year in which he'd observed at close hand the optimism and political imagination of the victorious nations disintegrate into renewed tension and paranoia, he decided that he had had enough. He asked for and received his discharge.

The orders for his decommissioning took time to process, and for several weeks Surry found himself without assigned duties. He used the time attempting to locate the two strange prisoners he'd processed in 1944, carrying out the search without really believing he'd find them. When he did find them, he discovered that they had created a small pocket of bureaucratic befuddlement. They were in limbo, and Surry recognized that if he didn't do something on their behalf, they might conceivably become permanent victims of the befuddlement they'd caused.

By coincidence, the Surry family estate was not far from the camp in which the two men were among the last half dozen inhabitants. The captain arranged for their release, and in June 1947, he took them to his family estate, where he intended to solve the mystery of their origin, and, if practical, to arrange for their repatriation.

•

The two men had enlarged their grasp of the English language in the nearly three years since he'd first seen them, although their vocabulary remained rudimentary and their understanding

---

articulate in giving expression to the truths about Cambodia. Sure, facts are recorded, events depicted, atrocities documented, statistics set forth—and their veracity argued over with great bitterness. But those who were in Cambodia over the last fifteen years may be unreliable precisely because they have witnessed its horrors at close quarters.

Why? Well, first of all, the personal witnesses have to live with their memories. Most of them, with good reason, have been scorched by the experience in a number of ways. Personal experience of extreme brutality makes clear thinking difficult for anyone. For the most part the witnesses were primarily professional journalists, and as such were being forced to operate as sensation collectors for the now-ubiquitous

of English syntax tentative. Yet in certain ranges of expression, their understanding had become quite sophisticated. Their ability to handle complicated abstractions was often surprising, so much so that Surry began to suspect that the limitations of their vocabularies were deliberate. Conversations with them began in the opaque, then would move only to the obtuse. Words like "sky" were within their lexicon, for example, but qualitative words like "clear", "cloud", "blue" and "weather" were not, nor did they show any inclination to retain simple descriptive concepts when they were introduced to them. The maps shown to them produced neither understanding nor curiosity; photographs of a variety of Asian locations invoked interest and a small degree of amusement, but no recognition.

After several weeks of frustration, Surry recognized that he could help them only by constructing a lexicon of *their* language—whatever it was. Once he had that, he could use it to pinpoint their origins and identities.

Taking on such a task was more than Surry had reckoned on. But the more he thought it through, the more attractive it became. The war had been a bitter disappointment to him. What had been taken on as a just war had degenerated into a return to the imperial aggrandizements that had set the stage for the war in the first place. Its lessons had not been understood by anyone in power, and he himself was no longer clear about what those lessons were. Finding the two men had delayed a decision he'd almost decided was inevitable: that the struggle

---

rewrite men at head office who shape and censor the observations of field reporters for the readers at home. Some of those who quit or went silent or were directly censored have since written memoirs. These memoirs have rarely been able to move beyond an undirected moral sensationalism. The result has been fifth-rate versions of *Heart of Darkness*—fifth rate because it is now not enough to expose *the horror, the horror*. After 100 million political killings horror is the fact one must now begin with. It is the one certainty. It must be penetrated, and its structural meaning exposed.

The prejudice for direct experience of a subject matter as a prerequisite for expertise is a revealingly modern one. In this circumstance, it is overrated and downright dangerous. I'm fair-skinned, extensively

against Facism contained no fundamental lessons for humanity, nor was the defeat of belligerent authority permanent. All that therefore remained to pursue was a life of personal gratification—satisfying the expectations of one's own family and class, or the demands of one's own senses. Now, unravelling the mystery surrounding these two men gave Surry renewed purpose. Perhaps the collapse into self-gratification was not an inevitability. Perhaps these men would reveal the ultimate truths the war had withheld.

At first the two men would not co-operate with Surry. In fact, they evinced extreme terror whenever he suggested he learn their language. For almost a month, they were mute whenever he attempted to get them to identify objects with their own terminology.

But by sitting with them and observing their conversations— something they did not object to and sometimes seemed to enjoy—he acquired one or two words. These he began to intersperse in their pidgin English conversations. Their initial response to this was fright, but when he persisted, fear turned to incredulity, then amusement. The process took several difficult months, but in the end they gave him the lexicon he required. A short time later, Surry had the answer to his puzzle. It didn't take long after that to piece together the tale of their travels.

●

---

if not well educated, a teacher, student, and an urban professional from a rural background. I even wear glasses. In Khmer Rouge Cambodia I would not have lasted a week, and I have few regrets that I'm not a journalist and that I have never been part of a military force. I have no circumstantial expertise. But I am no tourist, either.

Indirect experience I do have, and a couple of other qualifications. I'm an aggressive male of Anglo-Saxon descent, and my background taught me, among other things, the importance of being able to add two and two. I've rejected most of the mainstream values of my own society, not so much out of simple belief in the rightness of universal equality, but because I've developed an unrelenting hatred for the way Euroamerican civilization has wasted the immense wealth it has

The two men were Tibetan peasants. In the early 1930s, they embarked on a religious pilgrimage from the area around Yusho in Eastern Tibet to Lhasa. They were intent on entering a monastery—not an uncommon practice for young men in that culture. But early in their journey, as a result of an intense snowstorm, they became lost and wandered along the Dza (Mekong) river into Southeastern China, where they were captured by bandits. Shortly after their capture, the bandits packed up and marched into Northern China to join the Communists, taking the two young Tibetans with them.

From there, the two men escaped, and, after several years in which they probably skirted the northern lip of the Tibetan plateau, blundered into Central Russia, where they fell into the hands of the Russian authorities at Tashkent. The Germans had just invaded Russia, and the Tibetans were inducted into the Russian army and packed off to the Eastern Front as cannon fodder. Before long they were captured by the Germans—it wasn't clear whether by military misadventure or because they simply wandered away from their encampment and in behind the German lines.

Luckily, the German commandant involved in their capture didn't execute them. Instead, he had them transported to Poland, where they worked for a time in a concentration camp—Captain Surry couldn't determine which one it was, or its size, only that people were, in the words of the Tibetans, coming there "to the smoky light". But as winter approached, and

---

had. This could have been the earthly paradise. It isn't, not by a long shot, and I'm ready to find out why. And I'm tired of my armchair, both as a citizen and as an artist.

The Cambodians, as noted, themselves have been for the most part silent. Cambodian natives—Khmer or not—may take generations to move beyond the trauma of the decade between 1969 and 1979. Longer, since those events are either still under active revision or are politically and morally unresolved. The agony of Cambodia continues now that the country is under the control of the Vietnamese, who from the available evidence, seem to be offering the Cambodian peoples only slightly more dignity and self-determination than the Americans and the Khmer Rouge did.

under threat of the now-oncoming Russian armies, the concentration camp was dismantled and the two Tibetans were inducted into the German Army and transported to Normandy. There, as we know, once again they fell into the hands of a new authority.

Captain Surry went over the events again and again with the Tibetans, convinced that the riddle of their unlikely survival and their profound, elastic passivity in the face of hardship after hardship was eluding him. The modern world had done its worst to them, and yet had done nothing at all. The Tibetans were neither stupid men nor, on their own terms, were they ignorant.

Finally, it came to him. For ten years, these two men had believed that they were dead.

Reluctantly, the Tibetans confirmed his theory and elaborated. In their terms, their ordeal had been a test of their being, and a means, they hoped, of gaining *Nirvana*, however confusing and unorthodox those means were. They had survived because from the very first days they had believed that they were dead men caught in an unpredictable *Bardo*, or netherworld.

To the Tibetans, bodily survival had not been a goal, since they believed that they were already dead. They were traversing the netherworld in order to be reborn. They'd sought shelter, eaten and slept only because their bodies continued to make demands for shelter, food and sleep.

These demands puzzled them, as did the duration of their ordeal and its peculiar difficulties. After extensive discussion

---

The Americans, for all their vast cybernetic apparatus, are the least reliable interpreters. Skilled, well-intentioned and well-connected journalists like Jack Anderson remain Americans, at best caught up in the movement to heal their own wounded national dignity and confidence, and at worst, indulging themselves in the peculiarities of things American—hyper-erect manhood, the search for love and privacy, the pursuit of personal ambition and happiness.

I live in a country—Canada—that exists, somewhat uneasily, under the military protection of the United States. Canada is also the victim of American economic exploitation, and occasionally its partner in economic exploitation. Canadian cultural institutions are under siege by, and probably in the process of collapsing under, the pressures

and meditation they decided to respect these bodily demands—however bizarre—as aspects of the interrogations of their traverse of the *Bardo* plane. Indeed, they treated all the demands the same way, complying with every order and imperative that confronted them, always with the gravity and equanimity dictated by their understanding of where they were and what they were in search of. Their religious convictions told them that whatever the immediate consequences of being were, in the *Bardo* plane as elsewhere, the education of the human soul was all that mattered. And they were receiving an extraordinary education, one that they hoped would allow them *Nirvana*, or at least an elevated consciousness at rebirth. In short, every cruel barbarism perpetrated on them had, in their perception, an educative purpose.

Surry's interpretation was slightly different. During the war he'd seen that the survival instinct lodged at the core of the human organism carries its own logic. He believed that all being simply attempts to persist. Yet he did not argue his interpretation with the Tibetans, nor did he try to convince them that they were indeed normal living, breathing men in the same normal world they had been born into. Their certitude and inner peace convinced him of the absurdity of such argument. And he also recognized that to argue the logic of his Western sense of reality in the face of their experience of it would involve a greater absurdity. The evidence supported their view, not his.

---

of American electronic media. There are no bombs falling, and no deaths. But the shredding of our cultural fabric is as thorough as if it were being done by B-52 bombers.

We're nice people, Canadians. We have no military pretensions or ambitions, and our military traditions are minimal and decaying fast. There has been no military draft for forty years, and our armed forces have not seen combat since World War II.

In a sense, therefore, I have a relationship with the United States which carries elements of both American and Cambodian citizenship. And let's be clear. Cambodia may be my subject matter, but the United States and the Global Village is the source of the threat to my existence, and to that of almost everyone I will ever encounter. What

The Tibetans, ensconced in a large and comfortable rural mansion in a pleasant and suddenly peaceful country, admitted to a new confusion, one that they willingly discussed with Surry. They suspected that they had achieved an unpredicted and preliminary station of *Nirvana*. Surry understood the concept from his recent Buddhist readings. The Tibetans diffidently speculated aloud that this might be *Dharma-Kaya*, or birth-obstruction, but they could not explain this term further, except to say that the *Dharma-Kaya* was the real nature of that which is frightening. Wherever they had come to, its nature was as mysterious to the Tibetans as finding themselves in the *Bardo* plane had been from the beginning.

"We are ready," one of them told Surry in an attempt to explain, "for the Voidness bright by nature. We are confused here. *Karma* plays with our minds, as always. You are not a *Rakshasa*. When the *Rakshasa* tortured the souls for the Lord of Death, that we understood. We have seen the six lights of the world. Each many times. But where we are now is strange to us. We do not know which world this is, whether it is the *Deva* or *Preta* world. We know only that we cannot find the door."

This time Surry understood their confusion. The absence of predicted events and signposts explained their initial suspicions about his reification of their native tongue: they'd believed that their native language was the product of the land of the living. This latest confusion was similar. Nowhere in their knowledge of religious doctrine had the *Bardo* plane been depicted as a

---

better vantage point from which to understand the threat could there be than the one I already have?

•

The second question I ask myself is actually two questions. Both are slightly more specific. They have to do with the similarities between the ways in which the Khmer Rouge oppressed and exploited Cambodian citizens and the ways Africans were oppressed and exploited in the Congo during the administrative massacres of the Congo Free State: what are the economic benefits of genocide and why does the degree of barbarism grow with the degree of authority that exists?

pleasant place. And even the pleasantness was a source of confusion. There were no mountains here, no kin, no temples, indeed nothing of what they expected. Only the sky was familiar. The sky, with its changing light, was their only touchstone. In *Nirvana*, Surry had learned, there should have been no touchstones at all.

The Tibetans remained slightly uncomfortable with Surry's unceasing questions, but not profoundly so. Interrogations were part of the *Bardo* world. They accepted that. With short periods of grace, they had been questioned continuously throughout their pilgrimage. Surry's interrogations were by far the least painful ones they'd experienced.

With the mystery apparently solved, Surry began the arrangements that would see his two charges repatriated. A few days before they left, they recited a prayer to their benefactor, one that they told him they had repeated once every day from the very beginning of their journey. They offered it to the Captain with great solemnity, as a parting gift. Surry was careful to transcribe this prayer.

"Be lamps unto yourself," it went. "Be your own refuge always, and accept no external refuge. Hold fast to the Truth as if it were a lamp. Hold fast as a refuge to the Truth. Do not look for refuge to anyone or anything beside yourself. That man who is a lamp shall be a lamp unto himself, shall accept no external refuge, but holding fast to the Truth as his lamp, and holding fast as his own refuge to the Truth, shall by his anxiety

---

If my assumption is that barbarism has its roots within causalities more complex than "inherent evil", and that the heart of darkness is not a psychological event, then I had better locate barbarism at least partially within economic causalities. And here I run head on into an unexpected methodological problem. I've discovered, to my surprise, that the science of economics operates by faith.

This faith is created partly out of self-serving and self-generating rhetoric and partly out of an extremely covert metaphysics. In its precise theoretical definition, the science of modern economics undertakes only to determine the ways and means by which productive forces meet the demands for commodities made on them by society. It chooses not to discuss either the morality or the methods

to learn reach the very topmost height."

•

In the autumn of 1947, the Tibetans sailed for India. The journey was no doubt strange and wonderful to them, but when they docked at Bombay and set out on foot for Nepal and the gateway to Tibet, they were promptly caught in India's post-independence struggles.

On several occasions they were swept up in riots between Moslem and Hindu factions. They spent more than a year languishing in jails, and once came within a hair of being summarily executed. They faced these new trials with the same equanimity with which they had faced all the others; perhaps they faced them with greater calm. Captain Surry, when he put them on the boat at Southampton, assured them that they were going to what they had been seeking. He called it home, and they did not argue. He had spoken of mountains, and had named familiar names.

By 1952, they reached Nepal. They found work as menials, patiently saving what little they could in preparation for the last great event of the journey. Their life was not easy, despite their willingness to work hard, and their habitual asceticism. Several times they were robbed of their meagre savings, each time without complaining to the authorities. Yet when they'd accumulated enough to begin their journey through the

---

by which those demands are created and manipulated, nor does it undertake to widen its subject matter to the ecological and cosmological questions associated with mobilizing the vast productive apparatus of industrial civilization. It has no wisdoms to proclaim concerning the distribution of human wealth, and ostensibly, no opinion on the question.

Since all of the above matters are profoundly affected by economic activities—are, in fact, the functional sphere of economics—within that tight-assed academic refusal to widen its focus must rest a secret world: the covert, dark politics of post-industrial civilization. From the chasm between the exactitudes of academic economic theory and its vast and inhumane powers, from between the narrow theoretical edifice it

mountains, they did not leave, as one might have expected, and as Captain Surry had counselled them to do. Instead, they went into the Himalayan foothills, and stayed there until their supplies ran out. This pattern repeated itself several times.

In the summer of 1958, John Surry once again tracked them down. Surry's life, in the intervening years, had been governed by a single obsession. He had the story of the two men's wanderings, but when he sent them off to be repatriated, he had done so with a nagging sense that he had not understood their identities fully; that he had missed something essential.

Over the years, he pored over any Tibetan religious texts he was able to locate, looking for the missing pieces to his puzzle. In the process he ceased to be a Christian, yet without ever quite converting to Buddhism. But more and more he came to believe that his fate was contiguous with that of his two Tibetans.

Finally, in 1957, he made a discovery in the texts that convinced him that the two men would not in fact enter Tibet, but would instead wait on its borders searching for the womb-door that would allow them to be reborn. He quickly settled his affairs and left England on the first boat on which he could book passage. His intention was to take the Tibetans to Lhasa, where he would explain their pilgrimage to the Tibetan priests, and together with them, enter a monastery. In the spring of 1959, late in February, the three of them reached the Holy City of Lhasa.

The invading Chinese armies reached the city three weeks later.

---

declares as its portion of human reality and the twisted metaphysics of its actual range of control, the mind-choking darkness of the modern world may be issuing forth.

Thus, for instance, a nineteenth-century Belgian monarch can operate a vast economic *fascista* in which the covert by-product outweighs the intended product in exactly the same way an Asian Marxist government does in the 1970s. The sought-after commodity—rubber in the Congo, rice in Cambodia—was insignificant, or at least secondary. Production levels were minimal and the rice and rubber inefficiently produced. The by-product, which in both cases was the extermination of "inferior" or "undesirable" human beings, was achieved with stunning efficiency.

It is all too easy to stay in one's armchair and declare that human social structures, including those related to economics, must act in the service of humanity or be condemned as immoral or inhumane. What is more important than moralizing at this point in the analysis is to note that historically almost all economic structures have been "inhumane" because they are all indifferent to the value of consciousness in their analyses of productive processes. There are differences between one system and another, but only in degree, not in intended effect. Consciousness is the enemy of productivity in an industrial process. Marx, and those who have worked from his theoretical base, have been the only analysts in recorded history to actively suggest pragmatic alternatives to exploitive economics. But

The Kerrisdale Mission
for Destitute Professionals

I lost my job with the Planning Bureau around the time the recession started. It's okay. I don't mind talking about it. There's a lot of people who find any talk about the recession depressing. The world ended, they say, or Progress did. Well, dreams always end. People thought we could go on as we'd been doing for the last forty years, getting richer and bigger and fatter every year.

Those people aren't looking at it the right way. The recession was inevitable. The economy had run out of steam. The system was nearly bankrupt. If it'd been left to run it would have bankrupted every last one of us. I mean that literally. It may still, if we're not alert.

So now, things are different—times are a little tougher, people are a little meaner. No problem. You've got to roll with the punches, go with the flow. I mean, you know the saying—you can't fight City Hall. For a second there, I was going to say you can't argue with history, but I guess history is over,

---

his systems are unrecognizedly moral. Marx based his utopian solutions on a single metaphysical principle: that if social justice is achieved, the inherent political element in economic processes will disappear, and the state will wither away with it.

But in no instance—anywhere—has the state shown any inclination to wither away. On the contrary, the single unanimous phenomenon of all twentieth-century political systems has been the growth of state intervention and power—here in the West, in the Third World or within the Marxist sphere of control. And nowhere—not in the Soviet Union or elsewhere in the Marxist-influenced world—have Marx's utopian principles been applied so erroneously, nor failed so ironically and brutally as in Cambodia.

and it's back to the real world. We know we're not going anywhere.

The point is that we never were. It's delusionary thinking to expect things to get better and better. This is a practical world, not some socialist utopia. Utopian thinking is on the way out, and as far as I'm concerned, good riddance. I prefer reality. I'm addicted to it.

•

I remember how the Manager explained it to me the day he told us all our contracts weren't going to be renewed.

"We can't afford a long range planning branch anymore," he said. "The political boys have recognized that we're in a new kind of world. We can't afford long range plans when time has become an aspect of money transfer. So they're closing the Bureau. You boys had your fun for a few years, playing all those complicated policy-formation games with citizens. But the policy you created had a fatal flaw. It didn't provide the flexibility needed to operate in a high-velocity market economy. Flexibility is what is needed now. Democracy has to come to terms with the bottom line. If citizens want to participate in the political process they can do it at the ballot box, like they're supposed to."

That was my thinking exactly, but not everyone who got let go agreed. My colleague Leonard got pretty freaked out about

---

Before 1969, Cambodia was basically a peaceful—if nervous— agricultural society and economy, with some 90 per cent of its seven million people engaged in agricultural activities of one sort or another, the vast majority as peasant farmers. The country had maintained political neutrality since World War II, mainly through the strength and wiliness of its hereditary monarch, Prince Sihanouk. Cambodia was a net exporter of rice.

In four years, the American bombs and invasion destroyed that economy completely. By 1975, Cambodia was dependent on the United States for both its military and civil survival. Its two million refugees were living on American rice.

When the Khmer Rouge took control of the country, they emptied

---

it. And loud.

"Flexibility is a load of crap," he sneered. "All it means is that they want to run for cover every time a difficult issue comes up."

Leonard was my colleague for five years. He's a nice enough guy, but we'd never really been what you'd call friends. He's a little too cynical about the political process for my taste. No stomach for the bottom line. I couldn't help grinning when the Manager dropped right to that bottom line.

"No, they want flexibility so they can respond to development initiatives quickly and situationally," he snapped back. "We've got a sick economy here, and we can't afford to tie up incoming capital with red tape the way we once did. Not the way money moves these days. When an opportunity appears, you've got to tie it down fast or it'll run off to a more freeflow opening. There's no malice here, Leonard. Just common sense and reality."

Leonard hadn't quite got the message. "It doesn't strike me as common sense for a government to stop looking ahead and to lose track of how it got here," he mumbled to no one as he left the room. I say "no one" not because he was alone, but because no one was listening.

"It's over, Leonard," I told him. "Can't you see that? Give it up, or you're just going to damage your own credibility."

Me? I'm no cynic. I agreed with the Manager right down the line: the future is now. I'd had my roll in the gravy. Now it

---

the cities, evacuating the urban population and its refugees to rural collectives. The ostensible logic of the de-urbanization was sound enough, and it is unusual only in its extremity. Most revolutionary exchanges of political power, and almost all those that have involved civil wars, have seen a redistribution of population along with the redistribution of wealth. The Khmer Rouge explained to the world that the urban population was to be re-educated and purified, as a dozen revolutions had done before them. In most Marxist revolutions, re-education has been part of the revolutionary program, and in this sense, the Khmer Rouge were operating with "normal" boundaries.

But the ugly truth is that in Cambodia the concept of normality had been destroyed along with the cultural fabric and the economy.

was time to move on, keep up with the times. It might be tough going for a few months, but I was mentally prepared for it. When it comes right down to it, this isn't exactly Cambodia. The way I see it, the system is just jiggering its way back into kilter. If a few people get a kick in the wallet, that's tough. If an individual is alert enough, he'll survive and thrive.

That's my motto: *Survive, thrive, and be home by five.* We have to live in the present. It's okay by me. You can't argue with the will of the people, not if you want a share of the old pie.

•

I was able to negotiate a reasonably generous severance package, one that gave me six months clear to resettle myself. I knew it was coming, so the closing of the Bureau wasn't exactly a shocking surprise. I'd been thinking about what to do well before the announcement was made.

In the gravy days of the 70s, governments had more money than they knew what to do with, and all the opportunities were coming up there, in the public sector. Governments were dropping huge increases into social services, and even at that time I could see that a lot of the new services were superfluous— more than a few were just crutches to keep the young professionals coming out of the universities employed. As a matter of fact, long range planning was probably more helpful in keeping young professionals employed than for anything it

---

Cambodia was in the hands of an oligarchy of French-educated Marxist-Leninists thrust into power by the complete and unexpected collapse of a stillborn American-supported military dictatorship. Behind this inexperienced and untalented oligarchy were several hundred thousand psychotic guerrillas, most of them illiterate, under the age of twenty, and educated only to recognize and apply an authority based on violence and terror.

The task facing the Khmer Rouge was an enormous one. The Cambodian cities were enormously overcrowded, and agriculture in the countryside had all but collapsed from the predations of the 1969-1973 bombings and the disruptions of the liberation war. The country was facing imminent famine.

accomplished directly. Spending was a way of solving problems. Nice if you've got the money, but a hell of a thing to stop once it gets started.

Now, with the recession, governments are a lot poorer. A lot of the old solutions to problems have become problems on their own. We can't afford the social services we've already got. No way on this earth. People are going to have to drop all this nonsense about universal social justice, and get back to the competitive spirit—tapping the entrepreneurial energies that made this country what it is. I'm all for it. Let her rip, I say. And let me loose.

I covered all my options, naturally. I spruced up my C.V. and sent it out to every government agency I could think of, selling myself as a project expert. The pitch I made was vague enough to attract whatever possibilities were out there. But the more carefully I looked at the prospects, the fewer opportunities I could see to stay inside the civil service. So I set out to create a few opportunities of my own.

About that time, I ran into Jack Baxter. Jackie the Juice, they call him in the trade. Good luck comes to people who make it happen, and meeting him was a perfect example. He's an architect, and for the last decade he'd been greasing a variety of big projects, most of them inside jobs for government, usually building social housing.

Social housing, if you're not familiar with the term, was one of those wonderful scams the middle classes pulled off during

---

From the moment the evacuation order was given, the Khmer Rouge actions departed from any previous pattern. The apparatus of a modern state, even the most rudimentary institutions, ceased to exist. As if they were equating the Marxist canon about the virtue of the state withering away with the Western Civilization itself, they attempted to destroy all traces of it, and to thereby leap (backward) into utopia. Replacing it was something less than a civil state, and more: *Angka*—the Organization. It was raw, grinning authority itself. To be taken to *Angka*, to use the Khmer Rouge euphemism, was to meet death itself.

For those under the authority of *Angka*, "purification" meant summary execution, and "education" meant propaganda and violence.

the middle and late 70s, using the poor as a lever for getting their own housing subsidized. Mostly an inner-city phenomenon, and as with most things like that, it started off with the best of intentions.

The idea really originated with the big urban Social Planning Bureaus like the one I was part of. In theory, the idea was to artificially create an integrated social mix in new developments, which meant that the poor would learn how to be middle class by living in the same developments with people who had money. Great theory. In practice, most of the projects were actually subsidized through and through, and the people who had money got about the same long-term benefits as the ones without any money. And of course they got to bully the shit out of the poorer tenants, felt morally comfortable while they were doing it, and naturally they got the pick of the units.

Those developments did something else. They created an entire new class of poor—a working class with middle class values that make it impossible to admit or even recognize the poverty they suffer from. And there's another irony: while the middle class have been running their housing scams they've been developing their own poor anyway. So now we've got about 100,000 of them living under the flowerpots, as it were, wondering why they can't afford to go out every night and eat designer pasta and drink white wine spritzers with their friends. Aw. Ain't that sad.

I teamed up with Jack because he knew the delivery side of

The sole rite of purification available to the urban subject populations was death. Those who survived the move to the countryside and were able to elude the death sentences built into the biographical interrogations each person was put through—faced a life of constant subterfuge and slave labour. To admit that one had an urban past was to receive a death sentence. The slightest contact with the apparatus of modern civilization was a capital offence. To object to the most casual order was to risk being sent to a "Higher Education Centre"—a euphemism for being beaten to death. The Khmer Rouge cadres made no attempt to hide the fate of those who had been sent to *Angka*. Anyone removed from the communes in the evening was usually seeen dead on the trail to the rice fields the following dawn.

the development system through and through, and I knew the rest. We got to talking about what is going to be possible in the next few years, and what the government would be likely to put out for on the private/public sector interface. We both agreed that privatized contract provision of services would be the active area. That's when we got the idea of building a centre for destitute professionals.

Hey! Don't laugh. It's a real problem. The economic downturn at the start of the decade turned the burner up under a problem that'd been cooking right through the 70s: over-production of degree-carrying urban professionals. From the 1940s on, the ticket every government in the Free World sold to their citizens was the education-as-job-training ticket: do an M.A., do a Ph.D., get a high-salaried professional job, get a house and mortgage, get a Volvo wagon or a BMW. The promise was that anyone could achieve middle class security and the splendour of surburban living. The universities became factories for professionals. And of course, because front-loading systems always overproduce, we landed up with too many professionals.

Now that we're back playing social and economic hardball, a lot of these people are taking it on the chin. They aren't tough enough or smart enough to play hardball, and nobody ever told them they'd be expected to. Some of them get burned out and come apart trying to hold onto what they've accumulated. Others get pushed out of obsolete professions—like the one I

The atrocities committed by the Khmer Rouge are so brutal that it's easy for me to forget that I'm talking about the economic base of barbarism. The psychotic elements here are so spectacular that it requires a special effort to see the normative ones. And normative elements *do* exist.

One of the many macabre curiosities of the Khmer rouge period is the absence of data on its agricultural rebuilding programs. We know that large numbers of urban refugees were sent out under guard to reclaim abandoned agricultural tracts, to claim new lands from the jungle, or to build large hydraulic projects. Most of these projects bear a striking resemblance to the pseudo-scientific agrarian projects carried out in Russia during the 1920s and 1930s. The consequences

was in, and they fall flat on their faces. Their marriages come apart first, then they lose their homes and can't make the payments on their cars. Between you and me and the bedpost, quite a few of them are permanently on the skids, just like the bombed-out drunks down on Skid Row. It's an ugly problem.

Let's get right to the practical solution Jack and I worked out. Here's the salient elements of the proposal we presented, along with some of the working drawings:

THE PROBLEM:

There is a need to provide appropriate living accommodation and social services for the increasing numbers of chronically unemployed and/or burned out professionals. In order to meet this urgent social need, we are offering a project proposal and preliminary design that will house these unfortunate victims of societal update.

PROJECT RATIONALE:

Downward mobility is a socially and psychologically destructive experience for anyone, and one which urban professionals are uniquely ill-suited to cope with. It is important, therefore, in today's temporarily depressed job market for urban professionals, to avoid as far as possible subjecting them to the degrading realities of chronic unemployment. Those who unfortunately slip beneath the normative lifestyle habits and habitations of middle class life may not be reclaimable later on if they find their experience of deprivation too damaging. Hence it is crucial that they be enabled to retain the

---

of several of the Khmer Rouge projects have been witnessed. They were as disastrous and ill-considered as the worst of the Soviet experiments. Yet we do know that rice, cassava root and yams were successfully grown in the communes. We also know that the crops were harvested and then instantly removed. We also know that the process claimed untold numbers of lives. But we don't know if the deurbanization succeeded as an economic exercise in agricultural production.

Probably it did not, even though Cambodia is an extremely fertile country. The only measure we have is an inexact one taken by the Vietnamese after they invaded Cambodia during the winter of 1978-1979. They reported that the 1979 rice harvest yielded volumes

THE KERRISDALE MISSION FOR
DESTITUTE PROFESSIONALS

---

less than a fifth of the 1969 harvest.

A slave labour force is the least efficient of any work-force. Too many able-bodied workers have to be removed from the work-force to guard the slaves and keep them working. Human beings pushed beneath the level of minimal bodily subsistence have little productive energy, and the slaves find ways, in the horror of their condition, to withhold their productive energies. Leopold's experiment with forced labour in the Congo at the turn of the century captured pitifully small levels of rubber production given the numbers of "productive units" used and destroyed. The same was almost certainly true of the Khmer Rouge practice.

But maybe that is merely my hope. The human species is in deep

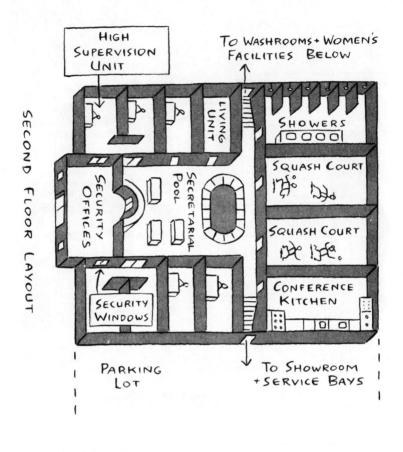

SECOND FLOOR LAYOUT

HIGH SUPERVISION UNIT

TO WASHROOMS + WOMEN'S FACILITIES BELOW

LIVING UNIT

SHOWERS

SECURITY OFFICES

SECRETARIAL POOL

SQUASH COURT

SQUASH COURT

SECURITY WINDOWS

CONFERENCE KITCHEN

PARKING LOT

TO SHOWROOM + SERVICE BAYS

trouble if methods to make forced labour productive are discovered. That is the goal of every totalitarian regime that has ever existed.

Perhaps, however, the point is being missed in this discussion of economic theory and agricultural production. The true "productive" goal in both the Congo and in Cambodia was the extermination of a human population; the true productive unit, death. Suffering and misery remain an unmeasurable and unharnessed quantity. At least their function and purpose remain fluid and undefined, despite their presence as a factor in every economic system. Managing or hiding them is the chief purpose of most economic rhetoric, and the metaphysics is almost solely an attempt to secure new ways to hide the inefficiencies and violence of the authority manipulating the

BED PULLS
DOWN

SECURITY
WINDOW

PORTABLE
DRESSER

CV
IN
OUT

TYPICAL LIVING UNIT

metaphysics. Authoritarian barbarism doesn't appear to have productive benefits. So far so good.

•

My third question has to do with Imperial powers. In the very recent past of Cambodia, and in Indochina in general, the chief Imperial actor has been the United States, with the Soviet Union and China playing Imperialist roles in the shadows of Vietnam and Cambodia respectively. Yet Imperial activities in Indochina have a long, ugly and international pedigree. The French were defeated and thrown out of Vietnam in 1954. Japan controlled the region for several years

lifestyle symbols and habits that previously made them social and economic assets to our society. The project has been designed to achieve those general goals through the following design objectives.

THE PROJECT OBJECTIVES:

  * *To create appropriate and comfortable living accommodations for chronically unemployed professionals.*

  * *To provide off-street parking facilities for the safe and dignified protection and storage of automobiles.*

  * *To provide appropriate social and recreational services.*

  * *To locate these facilities within areas in which clients will be comfortable and which will create and encourage client reintegration into society at the appropriate social level and wage scale.*

DESIGN VALUES:

  * *Project should be located in an area with appropriate income levels and social values.*

  * *Parking and auto storage areas should be tasteful, and if possible, unobtrusive. Aside from normal aesthetic considerations, this will enable clients to both protect valuable autos from the elements and to hide them from creditors during their period of economic disbenefit.*

  * *To provide clients with comforting imagery, individual units should be designed to resemble offices rather than living quarters. Beds should therefore be wall units, easily hidden from visitors. Units should be carpeted and provided with desks, telephones and computer*

---

during the Second World War, and before the period of French control that began in the nineteenth century, Imperial invasions of Cambodia came from Thailand, Annam and China. The Khmers themselves, and the Cham before them, were invaders. Right now, the Imperial equipment of Russia and China still contends in the jungles of Cambodia.

Imperialism, everyone agrees, is violent. In recent years, the level and intensity of its violence seems to be determined by the technological wealth and sophistication of the Imperial power involved. The more wealth and technological sophistication involved, the greater the violence. Marxists have traditionally argued that capitalism is the source of the violence. In the abstract, they are right. Capitalism is

terminals linked by a building-wide Unix system.

*   *Common recreational facilities should include meeting rooms and racquet sport facilities with shower and change facilities (this latter will obviate the need for washroom facilities within individual units).*

*   *The general design of the project should enable quick and cost-effective recycling should the present use of the facility become superfluous. The projected secondary use of the facility will be as a specialty automotive dealership, a use which would be highly appropriate to the commercial and market character of the area. It could also be sectioned as a modular consultant teleport, with most of its proposed facilities remaining unaltered.*

●

To make the boring part short, our proposal got a lot of quietly enthusiastic attention and the project was built. I'd already located a parcel of City-owned changeover land right in the heart of Kerrisdale, not more than a block from the City's ritziest nest of boutiques and restaurants. It was easy to make the City administrators see the project as "positive social amenity." They got behind it right from the start. An inside colleague of mine applied for and got a federal development grant, and under the City's new deregulated approvals process, helped along with a little hand-grease in the form of several key power-lunches, we had the facility on line before my severance package ran out.

---

based on exploitation and competition, both of which are inherently violent. But the Khmer Rouge barbarities were perpetrated by a Marxist-Leninist regime, and it isn't the first time a Marxist-Leninist revolution has gone that way. Notwithstanding, my first question here is this: to what degree is the United States responsible for the barbarities of the Khmer Rouge?

One of the truly horrific ironies here is that the U.S. military didn't really recognize the existence of Cambodia. The bombing of Cambodia was not directed at the Khmer Rouge, or even at Cambodia. The Khmer Rouge, in 1969, barely existed. The bombing of Cambodia was an attempt by the Americans to cut or destroy Viet Cong supply lines that ran through the jungle in the eastern part of Cam-

The City gave me a management contract to run the facility during the shakedown period, and I worked out a co-operative package between the university medical school and the Ministry of Human Resources. The university supplied a therapist two days a week, and the Ministry pre-screened clientele and assigned staff, including a recreational instructor and a retraining specialist.

One of the first clients to move in was my old colleague Leonard. After three months on the street, he'd had a nervous breakdown. His wife, a successful corporate lawyer, had put up with about six more weeks of crying jags and other loony tunes before she kicked him out. He'd been staying in the psychiatric unit at the university since.

Leonard had always been a troublemaker, and the moment he showed up I could see trouble was on the way. He had, as the saying goes, principles. I suppose that'd made him a good policy planner in the 70s, but he was finding out that his principles weren't much use in the high speed economic reality of the 80s. Sprinting is the name of the game these days, and you can't run very fast whle you're dragging a piano around and wanting to stop and play it every few minutes. To tell the truth, I wasn't too surprised to see old Leonard on my doorstep.

I was under a fair amount of pressure to make the facility run smoothly, as you can imagine. Jack figured that if this facility was a success, he'd have a leg up on designing the next ones. I could see my own opportunities in it too. If it went well, we'd

---

bodia. The invasion of Cambodia was undertaken with the same motive.

American tunnel vision about Vietnam had its roots right at the heart of American foreign policy. Consider then-Senator John F. Kennedy's 1956 explanation: "Vietnam," he said, "represents the cornerstone of the Free World in Southeast Asia, the keystone to the arch, the finger in the dike. Burma, Thailand, India, Japan and the Philipines, and obviously Laos and Cambodia are among those whose security would be threatened if the red tide of Communism overflowed into Vietnam." Laos and Cambodiia are almost afterthoughts to that list of "threatened" countries—so obvious that they almost go unnoticed. Or do go unnoticed.

have the franchise. It wasn't McDonald's, but it had the potential to keep both of us in hot tubs and Porsches for a few years.

Leonard started screwing around on the first day. Little things, you know, like he didn't like having to go down the hall to the washroom, and the curtains in his office were too sheer.

I told him that if he wanted a hotel, he should go down to Best Western. "This is an experimental facility," I said. "Why not try to be positive and help me work the bugs out of the system. If it's a success, we can build more of them for those who need them."

That shut him up, but not for long. The next complaint he had was about the recreational director, who he said was hogging the squash court for the people he happened to be teaching the game to.

"Look, Leonard," I told him. "Let's make this a co-operative venture. We've worked together before. We can do it again. I've only got a six-month contract here, and I'll be moving on. If you help me to get this system up and running smoothly, I'd be willing to recommend you as my successor."

I was lying through my teeth, of course. I wouldn't have hired that nitpicking loser to run a Kool-Aid stand. But it was worth a try.

Leonard didn't go for it. Negativity is a disease, I guess, and he had a progressive case of it. And he was a bit more cracked than I'd originally figured. He kept complaining, and stirring

---

We're talking dominoes here, but that worn-out metaphor fails to cover up the paranoiac relationship America had with the Viet Cong during the war. The exact sources of that paranoia are hard to locate because they are pervasive. Possibly they reside in the meeting rooms of the Pentagon: strategy sessions grounded in the lunatic logic of nuclear politics and guided by maniacs with the same values and psychological makeup as Conrad's Kurtz. Possibly they reside in the washrooms and coffee rooms of the same complex: bullshit logic grounded in machismo, overabundances of hormones, sexual inadequacies and racism. There, or in Congress, or across the coffee tables and barrooms of the country the Nixon presidency mirrored so perfectly.

up the other clients, a few of whom weren't exactly rays of sunshine either.

I made a few adjustments. I had a satellite dish installed on the roof, and piped it into the offices of whoever asked for access. It wasn't hard. The monitors on the Unix terminals were colour units, and one of the wizards down at the shop that installed the system figured out a way to access the dish through some simple keyboard commands. That satisfied a few of the malcontents who were bored with updating their C.V.s.

Leonard kept up his troublemaking, though. If it wasn't one thing, it was another. He was the worst, but he wasn't the only one. I was beginning to see that I'd underestimated the degree of morale breakdown that clients would be experiencing. I was sure about it the afternoon Leonard and a couple of his cronies burst into my office with a list of what they called "dis-equalities."

Their main accusation was a potentially dangerous one. They claimed that the facility offered no opportunities for relocation. It was, they said, half-way between a warehouse and a prison. Leonard called a reporter we both knew from our planning days, and he came as a witness when they dropped their list on me. I had to take the reporter out for an extremely expensive dinner to talk him out of writing a muck-raking piece on the incident.

The next morning I quietly introduced a system of restricted privileges. I also began to look into the idea of installing a master

---

There is a contemporary saying that all paranoia is justified. But in the political realm paranoia is a form of social and intellectual psychosis that breeds fear and secrecy. And fear and secrecy are the enemies of an open society. A common criticism of American intelligence operations during the Vietnam was that information was constantly being tailored to support the temporary political purposes of the bureaucracy guiding official policy, however temporary those purposes turned out to be. In reality, most of the American intelligence used was not intelligence at all, but self-propaganda. If, for example, American military commanders wanted to pursue a given course of action, their intelligence reports simply built a deductive phalanx of supportive data without analyzing the likelihood of the course of

locking system. I wanted one that could be activated on both individual units or building-wide. The City administrators objected on costing grounds, but when I made it clear just how much egg a disturbance would splatter on *their* faces, they pushed the budget requisition through in record time.

Leonard figured out what I was up to the day the specialists arrived, and that was when he made his big mistake. He tried to set fire to the place. That didn't work, of course. The sprinklers took care of the fire, and I got the medical people from the university in there within the hour to declare him a dangerous psychotic. They didn't want a big incident on their records either, so it was all done very quietly and *very* firmly.

I'll be damned if I know what he was really objecting to. His own case—prettied up a little—is a perfect demonstration of the need for this kind of facility.

Jack and I have three more facilities in the design stage right now. The security systems are beefed up considerably, and we have Leonard to thank for that. Jack joked that we should reward him with a retroactive consultant contract. I laughed, but not too hard. I'm not about to reward negativity, not even to joke about it. We've got a lucrative social issue on our hands, and I want it to stay right there for as long as it lasts.

---

action's success or failure from the data—thus reversing the definition of tactical intelligence, which is supposed to operate inductively.

One is tempted to agree with Hannah Arendt's contention that America cultivated its ignorance about the Viet Cong in particular and about Southeast Asia in general. It simply lacked any inductive impulse to its policy-making. But perhaps something else is going on. The United States possessed a conventional military apparatus meant to operate at a level of technological sophistication unprecedented in human history. With the exception of a few "primitive" societies (such as the Mayans, who had the wheel but chose not to use it) no society has been able to resist the use of technology once it had it. All technology, sooner or later, gets used to its absolute limits. And

technological capability breeds social and political ignorance by seem-
ing to replace knowledge.

An additional factor may be at work here. Technology, like
bureaucracy, is inherently politically conservative. Because the conservatism is inherent it is invisible to the practitioners of the
technology, if for no other reason than that it is always easier to operate
a mechanical device than to think about what it is producing and why.

Cybernetic technology is a step beyond mechanical technology, in-
asmuch as the operator cannot "see" electronic activity at all. Unlike
a machine, an electronic device resists intervention. Most electronic
devices are black boxes. Western political intelligence networks have
also become black boxes. Consequently, attempts to intervene in the

The Huxley Satellite Dish

Huxley is a small town on the coast of British Columbia, sixty or seventy miles from Vancouver. About two thousand people live in Huxley, most of them making their living by cutting down the forests, throwing the logs into the upper reaches of a river and then collecting them at the river's mouth. Other people from Huxley string the logs together and tow them a little farther up the coast to a pulp and paper mill where the logs are skinned, ground up, and made into grocery bags or items equally interesting and crucial to the safety and well-being of Western Civilization.

In Huxley they don't care much where things come from and where they go. The town itself was named after Thomas Henry Huxley, the English biologist, a disciple and sometime bulldog of Charles Darwin, but no one in Huxley knows that. If you were to tell them, they wouldn't be any more interested than if the town had been named after Thomas Henry's grandson Aldous, who wrote a book entitled *Brave New World*. Aldous Huxley took a lot of currently popular recreational drugs decades

---

U.S. network in the aftermath of Vietnam evoked peculiar and frightening responses.

What happened to Frank Snepp, a CIA operative in Vietnam who tried, in 1974 and 1975, to warn American authorities of the imminent collapse of the South Vietnamese military and government, and subsequently quit the Agency to write a book documenting the failure of American intelligence in Vietnam, illustrates what I mean.

Snepp's book, *Decent Interval*, was the subject of a landmark 1980 U.S. Supreme Court ruling that suppressed the book and placed a gag on Snepp and potentially on any other civil servant who might be seen to threaten the integrity and security of U.S. intelligence-gathering operations. The ruling entitled the government to seize all

before anyone else did, and he made some remarkably silly claims about their powers. No one in Huxley knows who either man was. They're both dead, aren't they? Like all that history stuff. What's so damned important about what's dead and gone, they'll say.

Rough-and-tumble outdoor people, the Huxleyites. They drink beer, smoke cigarettes without filter-tips, drive four-wheel drive vehicles and laugh a lot. A few of them live in those nice houses you can find in any suburb in North America, but most live in shacks and mobile trailers. On alternate weekends they drive into the mountains to ski or fish or they drive down to the city, where they shop in the big malls. Later on maybe they take their kids to the movies. Or at least they used to do those kinds of things.

Last year they changed. A few enterprising locals bought a T.V. satellite receiving dish and found a way to hook it into the local cable network so everyone in town could use it at no charge. Now, the people of Huxley, B.C. live in Detroit.

That's Detroit, Michigan we're talking about. Hub of the American auto industry. Home of the Detroit Tigers baseball club. Murder capital of the entire world.

Calling Detroit the murder capital may sound like an exaggeration. There are some cities in the southern hemisphere where more people get murdered, but that's different. Down there people murder one another over ideas, and all too frequently the government gets into the act along with them because they

---

of Snepp's profits from the book, and it imposed a *life-long* gag on him that requires him to clear literally anything he writes—even poetry—with the CIA. The Agency, under law, can remove any material it feels is classified or even classifiable—everything is potentially classifiable—thus allowing the possibility of literally every activity of the U.S. government becoming secret and confidential. More frighteningly, the ruling sets a legal precedent for suppressing any other civil servant in the same way, thereby preventing any possibility of the American system correcting itself from within.

That the U.S. has continued to repeat essentially the same mistakes it made in Vietnam in Iran and Lebanon and that it seems determined to repeat the mistakes in Central America supports Snepp's opinion

don't like political ideas. Nobody gets murdered in Detroit because they have ideas—least of all political ones. People in Detroit kill each other without giving a damn about politics. Just gimme that hot dog, gimme that wallet, gimme that woman. The spades in Detroit may hate the honkys and vice-versa, but when people get murdered it's supposed to be personal and not political, right? That's the North American way.

•

You may be wondering how hooking a satellite dish into a community cable system can land a small town in British Columbia in the middle of Detroit, Michigan. You probably suspect that I've made up the town of Huxley and its satellite dish to illustrate some silly idea I have about how horrible the modern world is, and why you shouldn't watch television. That being the case, you're either battening the hatches against an attack on your television viewing habits, or settling in to enjoy some interesting bullshit. Sorry to disappoint you. This is as real as the evening news. The only difference is that the definition here is going to be sharper.

•

For a few months after the dish was hooked in, nothing much seemed to change in Huxley. One thing that was noticeable was

---

that Vietnam has taught America nothing, but rather has severed its connection to reality altogether.

•

The collapse of the American-backed regimes in Indochina creates one set of increasingly ignored truths. But the aftermath of the Communist takeovers in those countries offers a different and yet-to-be-understood data set.

Vietnam is quantitatively and qualitatively different from Cambodia, and the two situations should not be confused. Against the most powerful military apparatus ever unleashed on this planet, the poorly

that the bar at the hotel experienced a sharp dip in business, particularly around dinner time. In the old days, people got off work and came down for a few beers before dinner. After the dish, only a few single men came in after work, and most of them left after one or two. Not many of them came back later, either.

The local stores had a slightly different problem. Merchants complained to one another that what had previously been their best hours were now the deadest, and that they were now busiest at lunch hour—their stores were filled with workers booking off for extended lunches to do their shopping. It was hard to get part-time help at lunch hour, because the high school kids weren't available, and none of the women seemed interested in working.

The reason for this was simple enough. Detroit is three time zones ahead of Huxley. What happens in Detroit at 8:00 p.m. happens in Huxley's future. Carson and the late movies go on at 8:30. And in the Global Village, three hours is a practical eternity, an entire prime time. A future. And who wouldn't want to live in the future if they could? The people of Huxley made their choice without second thoughts.

•

Living in the future gave Doris Klegg a very specific leg up in an important family argument. From the time Doris and her

---

equipped Vietnamese achieved political self-determination, decisively putting to an end the notion that direct political and economic imperialism can achieve its goals. This is the same lesson that Russia is currently learning in Afghanistan, and which the United States may soon have to relearn in Central America. And the Vietnamese may have to learn the same lesson in Cambodia. Maybe.

There was cause for optimism in what happened in Vietnam. There was even a reification of universal human truth: The human will to achieve self-determination apparently cannot be defeated. It can only be subjugated, suppressed and postponed. But ten years after the visible revelation of this truth, almost everyone feels uneasy about it. Why?

husband Herb moved out to Huxley, her sister-in-law Sue in Vancouver had let her know, and not very subtly, that she thought they'd moved to the middle of nowhere. Each time Doris and Herb visited her in Vancouver, Sue took pleasure in relating the details of her sophisticated city life, with its fine restaurants, its aerobics parlours, the better class of people, even the better selection of television programming available, things like the special sports and movie networks, or PBS and the local cable stations that provided extensive coverage of city events. One night after a few too many drinks, she actually phoned them up to tell them they didn't even *have* a lifestyle.

But with the satellite dish hooked up, Doris knew what went on in the world three hours before her sister-in-law did. She knew the plots of the soap operas and of *Dallas* and *Dynasty* before her sister-in-law did. Hell, when the Network ran a special movie about Mussolini, Doris knew what happened to him before Sue even started to watch. Doris racked up some hefty telephone bills demonstrating her new-found lifestyle superiority, but that was a cheap price to pay for living in the future.

•

Jimmy and Janet Wilson got married three months before the satellite dish. They were both local kids, fresh out of high school, and they got married because Jimmy got a full-time job in the

---

In the first place, Americans ought to have recognized this universal truth better than any nation. The American constitution, with its guarantees of the right to pursue happiness and its careful refusal to define the exact nature of that happiness makes it arguably the most sane political document the human species has yet produced. The problem is that successive American governments have studiously ignored it in their foreign policy, and Vietnam hasn't changed that.

Second, Vietnam may be unique. Between 1964 and 1974, the Americans dropped five or six times the amount of bombs on Vietnam than were dropped by all belligerents in World War II. The exact statistics are staggering. 14,400,000 tons of explosives were used, roughly half of which were bombs. Also used were some 400,000 tons

booming yard loading logs onto Japanese freighters.

Getting that job was a big confidence boost for Jimmy. He'd always been a skinny, shy kid. He'd be the first to admit he wasn't any genius, and right after that he'd tell you he didn't have the kind of personality that would get him a job as a host on one of those game shows he liked to watch. He felt lucky to have his job, and even luckier to have been able to marry a good-looking lady like Janet.

Janet's parents gave them the down payment on a house for a wedding present. The house was a new one, too, but it was in a subdivision nobody seemed to want to live in—maybe because it was next to the Indian reservation. Jimmy and Janet liked the house just fine. Jimmy's parents bought them a 26-inch RCA colour television for a wedding present. Jimmy bought a waterbed, a dresser, and a couch from one of those chain discount stores in Vancouver, and he scrounged a kitchen table and some chairs from a trailer someone had just up and walked away from. They were making do for the rest of the things they needed. Times were getting tough in the logging industry and a lot of folks were moving back east where the jobs were more plentiful, so household goods came pretty cheap.

Jimmy and Janet weren't in a hurry to do anything or get anywhere. They liked life in Huxley. They had everything a young couple needed. He had a secure job, they had a good house and a top-rated television, and when the satellite dish started operating, it gave both of them a sense of the finer things

---

of napalm and nearly 19,000,000 gallons of herbicide, of which more than 11,000,000 were the deadly Agent Orange. Also used were 170 kilograms of Dioxin—not a large amount until one realizes that this chemical is toxic to life in *parts per billion*.

Against this the Viet Cong and the North Vietnamese countered with a degree of organization and dedication that is quite simply without parallel in human history. Theirs was a fifty-year struggle, one that had achieved partial success in 1954. Only that degree of dedication could have withstood the high casualty rates within the communist cadres; annihilations were the rule rather than the exception. Few of those within the Viet Cong ranks in 1964 were still alive when the war ended. Underneath that the Vietnamese have a thousand

in life, as fine as anything they'd get in Vancouver or anywhere else. Jimmy came home right after work each day and he and Janet watched the prime time programs with supper, sitting on the couch. They were in bed by 9:30 at the latest, after Carson and maybe a little hanky-panky. Janet wasn't pregnant yet, but she was already putting on quite a few pounds.

•

Huxley was changing too. From the inside the changes weren't easy to see—the town didn't look any different, unless you were driving down the deserted main street after 9:00 p.m. But since few people in Huxley were out at that late hour, nobody thought much about it.

Other changes were similar. Huxleyites went into the city just about as often as they did before, but few of them did much except shop. Vancouver just didn't seem quite as exciting as it used to. It wasn't a very big city, and now it had a kind of foreign feel to it.

Even fewer Huxleyites went skiing and fishing. There was more baseball in the summer, and the winter after the dish started up the high school gym got taken over by people wanting to play recreational basketball. A motion was made at City Council the following spring to fund the construction of some outdoor halfcourt basketball facilities. The motion received swift assent: it would give local kids something to expend their

---

year history of resistance to Imperial aggression that dates prior to Le Loi's success in driving out a huge Ming invasion force in 1427. Vietnamese militarism is ingrained; even inbred. In the decade since the liberation of South Vietnam from American control, there has been no liberation of the Vietnamese people from the psychological burden of militarism, and there has been no celebratory renewal of human rights.

But we have to be careful with our condemnations. As in Cambodia, partial evacuation of the urban areas occurred in Vietnam during the war's aftermath. In Vietnam, urbanization had been a deliberate American policy—an attempt to deprive the Viet Cong of support and recruits by bringing the population into the government controlled

energies on.

Over at the high school, the principal was mildly disturbed by the formation of two tightly organized and competitive social groups among the students. He didn't care for the change in student dress patterns, either. The kids had taken to wearing leather jackets, denims and sneakers no matter what weather conditions prevailed. The two groups wore what they called "colours", jackets with crudely drawn pen markings, often with obscene slogans. He also noted the appearance of tattoos on both male and female adolescents. That one he reported to the School Board.

More disturbing to him was that the two gangs appeared to be aligned racially. About thirty percent of his students were native Indian, mostly coming from the reservation that adjoined the town. He'd always maintained that as Indians go, the Huxley band was a pretty progressive lot, and he'd been an enthusiastic supporter a few years back when the band leaders petitioned the Government to extend the television cable system into the reservation. He wrote a letter saying that the Indian band had as much right as anybody to enjoy the fruits of modern technology and its cultural amenities.

Up until recently, there'd been very little racial tension between the white and native kids in the school or anywhere else in town. If you worked hard and could hold your liquor, people would think you were okay even if your skin was green with purple polka dots. Now Indian and white kids weren't even

---

cities or by concentrating them in "strategic hamlets" that were often far from the rice fields and far from their native area. As late as 1964, 80 per cent of Vietnam's population was rural. By 1972, only 35 per cent remained in the countryside. De-urbanization in Vietnam was therefore a necessary program, and a long-term undertaking that is presumably still going on.

Yet within months of the fall of Saigon on April 29th, 1975, the actual situation began to grow cloudy. It is relatively certain that the liberation period and the de-urbanization process in Vietnam did not remotely resemble what happened in Cambodia. The discipline of the conquering army alone ensured that. There was minimal looting by the army, and apparently little revenge-taking.

talking to one another.

Another thing that disturbed the principal was the lack of interest in the kayaking club, long a fixture at the school. The principal was an avid kayaking enthusiast, and his main reason for moving to Huxley, years before, had been the abundance of first-rate kayaking streams in the area. Over the years he'd taught hundreds of youngsters the skills of the sport. For the first time, not a single student had signed up for the club, nor could he coax or cajole anyone to apply.

People stopping in town noticed the changes. The easiest things to spot were the unusual numbers of people wearing Detroit Tiger baseball caps; *Magnum P.I.* fans, they guessed. But then they saw the paraphernalia of the Lions, Pistons and Red Wings. That caught the eye of an investigative reporter by the name of Chuck Cambridge. Chuck worked for a Vancouver television station and he stopped into Huxley on the way back from a fishing trip upcountry. He thought it curious enough for a novelty story, and a week later he returned to Huxley with cameras and a crew.

•

Chuck decided to talk to the kids first. He figured they'd be more open; he knew that they'd been raised on television, and that they'd be more spontaneous with cameras around. But he couldn't find any young kids on the streets. They were inside,

---

But then former south Vietnamese army officers were taken to camps for what were promised to be thirty day "re-educaton programs". Up to that point there had been no apparent reason to fear the new regime or its army. Both sides seemed relieved simply to have peace at last. Most of the army officers went willingly. Most did not return.

Since then, information has leaked out slowly but steadily, and most of it is depressing. The National Liberaton Front (NLF) and the Provisional Revolutionary Government (PRG), which together were the political arm of the Viet Cong, were disbanded and many of their leaders supplanted by North Vietnamese party cadres. In the process it became clear that the NLF and the PRG were not, as had been

he discovered later, watching Mickey Mouse club reruns or the cartoon channel. The older kids were around, but they weren't interested when they discovered he wasn't with MTV, the rock video network, and that he wasn't offering money or prizes. He did record one conversation with a group of denim-clad native kids who were standing around a 7-11 store just outside the reservation.

"I'd like to talk with a few of you for a moment," he said, clambering out of the truck and popping his I.D. card at them.

A heavy-set youth, obviously the leader, ignored him, and walked over to the cameraman who'd gotten out with Chuck and had trained his camera on the group. The leader placed his hand over the lens, smearing its surface with his fingers. "Say what, man?"

"Could you please remove your hand from in front of the camera?" Chuck asked, politely. "I'd like to film your entire group."

The leader's hand stiffened around the lens in a crudely threatening gesture. "I'm the dude does the talkin', man," he said. "You wanna talk to the Chieftains, you talk to the Man."

"Fine with me," Chuck squeaked, thinking that maybe he should try to sound more like one of those MTV hosts the kids watched. "Hey! You're the action here. You're the news."

The leader stepped back, and hitched his thumbs in his belt loops while Chuck's cameraman rearranged his equipment and focused in. "Hey man. Which station you working for?" the

---

projected by American intelligence, composed solely of Marxist-Leninist revolutionaries, but were what they'd always claimed to be: broad-based organizations seeking national liberation. The non-Leninist elements of both were simply and quietly suppressed between 1976 and 1978, and Vietnam was unified as an authoritarian Soviet satellite state.

Here, however, data disappears again, and one is into a realm of speculation. One speculation that hasn't received much attention is that Vietnam may continue to be different from anything on the planet. No one knows what the effect is, ecological and genetic, of having 19 million gallons of lethal herbicides dropped on an area the size of California. Common sense suggests that there have been effects, and

leader demanded.

Chuck identified his station.

"Never heard of it. You from Detroit or Dearborn?"

"Vancouver."

"Vancouver?" the leader sneered, raising both hands to the sides of his head and snapping his beaded Adidas headband in a gesture of contempt. "Vancouver's noplace. Chieftains don't talk to cameras from Vancouver. Get out of my face, y'hear?"

•

Chuck interviewed Doris Klegg. She was more accommodating. She knew that her sister-in-law would probably see the interview, even if no one in Huxley would. Doris tried to be philosophical, but it was hard to hide the pride she felt about living in Huxley, in the future. She said a few words about what it was like knowing things before people in Vancouver did, and she talked about how wonderful all the new technologies were.

Chuck was bewildered. "You know," he told her just a little sternly, "that things really happen at the same time everywhere. You're just on a time advance. Detroit's time zone is three hours ahead, that's all."

Doris gazed back at him, calmly superior. "Of course. That's why we get all the important programs three hours before you get them. It doesn't matter when things happen, anyway. It's when people find out about them that counts. And we know

---

that they're almost certainly profound effects—be they ecological, genetic, or economic and socio/political. If there are no effects, then every ecologist worrying in public about the effect of chemicals in the environment is an hyperbolist or an outright liar. Western apologists returned from visits to model communes in the new Vietnam telling apocryphal stories about how the Vietnamese were recycling the twenty-five million bomb craters as fish-ponds. The peasants were said to be poor but happy, and the rice harvest was apparently returning to acceptable levels. These stories may be true. At least they didn't fill the bomb craters with corpses, as they did in Cambodia.

It may also be the case that large sections of Vietnam are ecologically dead, and that it was this situation, and not humane considerations,

about everything three hours before you do."

He left Doris's place shaking his head. A small part of him was wondering if maybe she didn't have something. After all, the national news did come from Toronto, and it *was* broadcast three hours late in the west.

•

Doris suggested that he drop over to Jimmy Martin's place. Jimmy, they said, watched more television than anyone in Huxley since he'd been laid off in the booming yards three months back.

Jimmy was watching *Detroit Today* when Chuck arrived, but he invited the crew in anyway.

"This'll be over in ten minutes, so you guys can set up while I finish watching this," he said, waving Chuck and the crew inside. "There's an hour of reruns between five and six. I can talk to you while those are on. It's actually ten to five in Detroit," he added. "Here too."

"The little woman's asleep," Jimmy explained to no one in particular. "She can't watch as much as I do. Oh, she gets up to catch the cooking programs and a few of the early soaps, but she sleeps most afternoons, and she goes to bed before the late movies start."

"How much television do you watch on an average day?" Chuck asked, signalling that he wanted the camera rolling.

---

that led the Vietnamese to invade Cambodia in 1979. Quite simply, the Vietnamese may need Cambodia's agricultural capacity to feed its own population. They may also have deliberately held off the invasion while the lunatic Khmer Rouge regime reduced the number of Cambodian mouths that needed to be fed. We just don't know.

•

In Cambodia, the Americans had no policy and no program. In Vietnam they splashed herbicides and napalm on jungle and agricultural lands alike in a *de facto* attempt to destroy the capacity of the Vietnamese to feed, clothe and shelter themselves. But in Cambodia, they

Jimmy relaxed into the couch and pulled his feet up onto the plastic milk crate that served as both footstool and coffee table. "Oh, I don't know. About twelve hours most days. But I can go up to fourteen or fifteen on a good day. Janet only watches seven or eight. Sometimes nine if I push her."

Janet appeared, bleary eyed. She sat down heavily beside Jimmy and stared at the television set. "What's going on?" she asked.

"Nothing much," Jimmy answered, without looking at her. "These guys came up from Vancouver to do a story on the dish. Someone told them we watch quite a bit, so they came over here."

"Oh," she said. "Anything interesting on?" She reached across Jimmy and changed the channel. "*M.A.S.H.* is supposed to be on channel 42 at five. Anything interesting later tonight?"

"The usual," Jimmy said, stretching out on the couch indifferently.

Chuck moved in on Janet. "How do you feel about the satellite dish, Janet?" he asked. "Has it improved your life here?"

Janet gazed up into the eye of the camera lens like a fish contemplating a baited hook. "Oh, sure," she said, brightly. "It's a lot better. There wasn't really anything to watch before the dish. Just five or six channels, that's all. Really primitive."

"Doesn't all the programming about Detroit bother you? I mean, this is British Columbia. Detroit is a long way away."

---

began by bombing the Viet Cong, not Cambodians. When the Khmer Rouge began to appear in numbers, the Americans overthrew the Sihanouk government and installed and armed a military dictatorship right at the time that they were withdrawing their own troops. The refugees who fled to the cities were the victims of military actions, not of any considered policy on anyone's part.

The policies of the Khmer Rouge were both unorganized and genocidal, based more on the will to exterminate the urban populations than to solve the problem of artificial urbanization created by American bombings and their own military operations as they advanced toward victory. Their fears of renewed American bombings (one of the excuses given at the time of the evacuation of the

Janet's expression grew serious. "I don't know. I don't mind it. I mean, Detroit's real enough."

Jimmy interrupted. "Life is the same everywhere now. The prime time lineup is just about the same wherever you go. Since we've had the dish we get more choice, that's all."

"How many channels do you get?" Chuck asked.

"Gee," Jimmy said, momentarily nonplussed. "I've never really counted. Some of them are clearer than others. But there's enough so there's always something interesting to watch. You just keep flipping until you find what you need. There's no need to count channels."

"I understand that you lost your job a few months ago," Chuck asked, feeling sly and investigative. "How does that make you feel? Are you worried about the future?"

Jimmy shrugged. "Yeah, that's right. I did lose my job. But look. I don't worry much. The dish helps. It fills up the time. And something will turn up. Janet's thinking of getting pregnant, you know, and I'd just as soon be around for that anyway. Something will turn up," he said, this time a little more blandly. "Maybe something in the auto industry. You may not know about it, but things are looking up these days in the industry."

●

Chuck Cambridge did several more interviews before he left Huxley. The owner of the Huxley Motor Hotel said that he'd

---

cities was that they feared the Americans might use nuclear weapons on them) might well have been sincere enough in some quarters. But the Khmer Rouge, as an organization, was conceived and built out of political, social and technological insanity. It existed in a state of permanent psychosis. It believed that the urban populations were hopelessly perverted by their civilized experience, and therefore poisonous.

Arguably the Khmer Rouge may have *been* a psychosis created by American military actions inside Cambodia. The Americans bombed and invaded Cambodian territory, killed several hundred thousand people and disrupted the lives of millions more. But from beginning to end they treated their actions as a side-show to the war in Vietnam.

considered putting his entire business on Detroit time. He'd decided against it because the tourists would have found it confusing. And tourists had become an increasingly important part of his trade now that the bar wasn't doing the local business it once did.

"People here just don't go out like they used to," he said, looking a little wistful. "They drink at home now, in front of the television. And goddamned if I can blame them, with all the programs we've got to choose from. I guess there's a part of me that wishes the dish had never been installed. If things don't change it's going to put me into the poor-house."

The high school principal trotted out the predictable authoritarian concerns about the collapse of school discipline, but he didn't seem to object to the dish even when Chuck prodded him to say something hostile.

"This is modern life, I guess," the principal said. "When things change, a few good things are lost. That's progress. As an educator I can't object. It's my job to teach Huxley's children how to live in the real world, not in the past, however comfortable I may find it."

He went on to mention the school's new communication program, and when Chuck said he wasn't sure what that was, the principal told him that he'd voluntarily cancelled the school's library acquisition budget and had put the funds into educational video.

"The students are much more comfortable with video

They likewise treated the emergence of the Khmer Rouge as a phenomenon subsidiary to the existence of the Viet Cong, and assumed that the Khmer Rouge were under Viet Cong control.

The Vietnamese also responded peculiarly. They provided the Khmer Rouge with weapons, but made little attempt to influence or assist them after the war ended. Sure, they had their own problems to deal with. And maybe they saw the mass psychosis at the heart of the Khmer Rouge. Even when they invaded in late 1978, the Vietnamese made no serious effort to wipe the Khmer Rouge out. They simply pushed the defeated remnant back into the jungle without negotiating with them or trying to reconcile their differences. They then carefully blamed Khmer Rouge excesses on Pol Pot and his

materials," he said. "And it makes the teaching loads easier as well. The School Board is getting us three microcomputers, so we'll be up to date on that sector as well. We're looking to be front and centre on the future."

•

Just about everybody in Huxley was positive about the dish, except for some old English duffer who said that it was destroying the town and everyone in it. Chuck was a thorough investigator; he filmed the duffer's side of it too, even though the old boy wasn't too specific about why the dish was so destructive. Whatever it was he had to say got edited out of the four-minute story on Huxley that was run late in the Vancouver station's news hour a few days later.

A few people in Huxley tuned in to watch it, but Vancouver's news hour fell into the middle of prime time. *Dallas* was on, and for most Huxleyites who remembered Chuck's visit, the choice was an easy one to make.

•

About three weeks later someone tied a couple of sticks of dynamite to the base of the dish, and right in the middle of *Miami Vice*, the explosion scattered the dish and half the cable-vision office across the main street of Huxley. The local police

---

Chinese backers, assiduously side-stepping the fact that both regimes were organized around the same Marxist-Leninist doctrine.

There are still at least 25,000 Khmer Rouge in the Cambodian jungles, harassing the Thais, Vietnamese, and the puppet Cambodian administration alike. They are provided with military support by China, and in a bizarre twist, are tacitly supported by most Western governments. They sit in the United Nations as the representatives of the Cambodian people to this day. No doubt they also receive some covert military and economic aid from the West. We are in collusion with them. Every damned one of us. It is a collusion of ignorance and indifferent exploitation that is as dark as the Stanleyville Station.

investigated, and before too long, they traced the dynamite back
to the owner of the Huxley Motor Hotel. Who knows why he
did it. Maybe it was the interview with Chuck Cambridge that
got him thinking.

The corporal of the Huxley RCMP charged him with the
crime, but the case never did get to trial. The night after the
charges were laid, a group of the locals entered the hotel bar
around 10:00 p.m., and after drinking for an hour or so, they
wrecked the place. What happened after that isn't clear. The
owner simply disappeared.

There were rumours, predictable ones. One of them was that
when the owner left the premises around one in the morning,
somebody put a knife between his ribs and then dumped the
weighted body into the river. Another rumour had it that he'd
been, ah, encouraged to leave town, and pronto. His car
disappeared with him, so that was the story the local police
accepted, and a warrant for his arrest was put on the electronic
wire. It was Huxley's first All Points Bulletin, which made the
corporal feel quite proud of himself but didn't result in an arrest.

The Vancouver television crews showed up again, but this
time no one in Huxley was talking, at least not about the owner
of the hotel. The leader of the Chieftains did say that his people
didn't have anything to do with it but that he thought that the
bastard had got what was coming to him. "Go talk to the
honkys," he said. "The hotel's on their turf."

It took six weeks to replace the dish and the damaged cable

8

Imagine a crowd of people arrested merely for being, in the judgement of some powerful official, in too-great numbers in a given location. The innocents—now prisoners—are locked into insufferably
cramped quarters, and during the night, half of them suffocate or die
by other means. The same official who casually ordered their detain-
ment has gone home in his silver Mercedes-Benz, to dinner and to
the attentions of his wife and servants. He has just as casually forgotten that he has given the order to have them imprisoned.

The official goes to bed late, and although slightly drunk, he sleeps
soundly. Early in the morning he is awakened by a panicky aide. The

system. The community really came together to get it fixed, and they paid the cost out of their own pockets to keep the Feds from coming in and busting them for having a dish illegally hooked into a community system. They had a benefit dance to raise funds, and even some of the Chieftains put aside their hostility toward the white community and danced up a storm. The new dish was hooked back into the Detroit network, and in a few days, life was back to normal.

official, the aide announces respectfully, has an administrative problem on his hands, and he desires instructions on what is to be done. The administrative problem arises not from the deaths of the prisoners but from the fact that a member of the Western press has gotten wind that a spectacular number of citizens have died under unusual circumstances. The cameras and newsmen of the Global Village are on their way.

At a press conference later the same day, the official calmly announces to the assembled newsmen that the detainees, who in actuality are members of one of a number of tribally-oriented quasi-political factions active within the country, are in his governance of fact, members of a leftist terror group, and that their demise is the

Malcolm Lowry and the Trojan Horse

Let me begin with some declarative statements: The Trojan Horse was the most remarkable device built by the Mycenaean Greeks, and it is among the most devastating inventions in the history of language. Language is the most profound of all human inventions; the most flexible one, the most commonly used. It is our most carelessly maintained invention, and because of that, it has always been the most dangerous one, both to its users and to the planet.

Wait a minute, I hear you saying. Never mind the grand generalities. The Trojan Horse wasn't a linguistic invention. It was a cunning technological device constructed by the Greeks in order to breach the walls of Troy and win the war; a piece of trickery. The only unusual linguistic element in the story was that the Greeks concealed inside it stopped arguing among themselves long enough to fool the Trojans into dragging the Horse inside the walls of the city.

Try looking at the Trojan Horse in a different way. First of all, it was the invention of Odysseus, the most cunning of the

---

result of water-poisoning by a competing terrorist organization. Unfortunately there are no witnesses to corroborate what he tells them. Those who survived the ordeal have been disappeared.

The camera crews from the Global Village are allowed to film some of the corpses, and the official, dressed in a Western business suit, gives interviews to all takers, explaining in several languages, and with a shrug of resignation that can be recognized universally, that he and his government have tried to keep order, but that failure is a fact of life in the "developing nations": progress is gradual; it will not come without extensive foreign aid.

The incident, and the interview that "terminates" it, could easily be the subject matter for an essay by V.S. Naipaul or scenes from

Greek warrior chieftains. To invent the Horse, he had to put his mind in two places at once. This had never been done before.

In those days, human beings still thought of themselves as part of nature. In order to conceive a trick like the Trojan Horse, Odysseus had to create (and operate) the concept that human consciousness is an entity distinct and separate from nature—outside its laws. By doing this, he transformed the gods that both the Greeks and Trojans worshipped. Instead of embodying aspects of nature, the gods became aspects of individual consciousness. Psychologisms—daemonic or educational. For Odysseus, the god represented by the Trojan Horse was a tool.

That may not sound very tricky to you, but to the Greeks and Trojans before Odysseus, it was, literally, unthinkable. And if you examine it carefully, you'll see how complicated it was. Everything Odysseus did involved the manipulation of abstractions: mind, divinity, the horse itself—things that were not at all abstract to his people. Again, easy for us. But for them, material reality—objects, processes, people—were inseparable in those days, part of a continuum linked by the metaphors of nature.

The Trojan Horse was therefore (at least initially) a philosophical invention, the first of its kind. It was dark and empty inside—rather like most modern philosophical metaphors. As a physical object, the Horse may not have existed in the form and size to which legend has elevated it. Possibly the Greeks built a small and beautiful icon, or used a real horse and then

---

one of his novels. It could also be the substance behind one of those two-inch newsclips the morning tabloids are filled with. If you're not sure what I'm talking about, try counting the number of deaths the tabloids enumerate each day but leave totally unexplained.

Naipaul's work frequently suggests that the casual violence of the Third World—the darkness—has its sources neither in deliberate cruelty nor in lack of education, but in thoughtlessness. This, ultimately, is the most damning accusation a colonial can make to himself or to others: *to be without thought*. Personally, I don't register the particulars of this paradigm easily—my own political and social experience has been much less violent, or violent in different ways. But I do recognize, absolutely, the terror of it, because like Naipaul, I am a

approached the portals of Troy at a time of common festival rites and asked permission to offer sacrifice to the divinity. The Trojans, believing in the then-inviolable reality of metaphors drawn from nature, assented to the request, unable to imagine that the Greeks would be capable of collective blasphemy.

To the Trojans (and to the Greeks up to this point) blasphemy was possible by individual error or accident, or by willful perversity. But never in cold blood and never as a political tactic. For the Ancients, political tactics were more limited than they are now. There were the tactics of battlefield geometry, and the deceptions practised between one person and another that are as old as the human species. But nothing like this.

I'd dearly love to ask Homer about the Trojan Horse, but he's been dead for several thousand years and he spoke a language I don't understand. Besides, Homer himself (or herself as the case quite possibly is) is a metaphor for the uncounted oral transferences of the cultural myth of the Trojan War from one Greek to another, and for the much later act of writing down the collected intelligences of those voices.

That being the circumstance, I've looked around to find a modern and nearby equivalent of Homer. Luckily I've found one quite close to home: Malcolm Lowry, the Homer of alcoholic writing.

Again you complain. This time you accuse me of cruelty. Malcolm Lowry was a great writer, a tortured man.

No argument there. Malcolm Lowry was a great novelist. He

---

colonial.

Colonials are no longer common. In fact, they have become a rarity. The majority of people in the Third World are no longer colonials. Few seek entrance to the Imperiums, Marxist or Western. Most Third World countries are nominally self-governing, if still economically dependent and in debt, and those of their people with political power have their own personalized imagination of a new kind of Imperium. Some of those without power may have a hunger for the orderliness of the old Imperium, but most merely have hunger. Third World political visions—to be promulgated by the communications apparatus of the West—are now, generally, idealized versions of the societies the Imperial conquerers clubbed into submission over the last four

wrote one great novel: *Under the Volcano*. He also wrote several very bad novels, all of them, like himself, beloved of hard drinkers across the English speaking world and beyond. Lowry was also a first-rate drunk. Arguably, he was better at drinking than at writing. It's fair to say that he worked harder at drinking, and that in the end he was more loyal to that technology of altering consciousness than to those normally associated with writers. But since Lowry's capacities for both were magnificent, and because we are discussing both the alteration of consciousness and the possession of two minds, I decided he might have something interesting to say about the Trojan Horse. Several years ago, I began to search for him.

Another howl of derision? Yes, I'm aware that he's been dead for years. So what? This is fiction, remember? I can do anything I want. If Kurt Vonnegut can take us halfway across the galaxy for a few cheap intellectual party tricks, I can take you to Gabriola Island, which supplied part of both the title and the subject matter of Lowry's last novel, *October Ferry to Gabriola*.

●

Lowry's problem was that the impulses that made him write were the same ones that made him drink. Written English sentences probably offer greater possibilities for ambiguity than those of any language in human history. For sure, the sentences Lowry wrote were simultaneously opulent and labyrinthine.

---

hundred years. The Third World wants those old societies reified, but in low-density images, with modern military ordnance for the police and army, and enough colour television sets to keep their up-wardly mobile classes dazzled.

I do not come from what is normally regarded as the Third World, but that doesn't matter. I am still a colonial—perhaps the only kind left. In the latter part of the twentieth century, a colonial is one who retains a fundamental imaginative relationship with the Imperium. For us the Imperium is the libraries, museums and galleries of London, New York, Paris—the repositories of Western Civilization's attempts to achieve self-understanding and civil harmony through the re-enactment of what is beautiful or profound in life.

When they did what he intended them to, they were symphonic-ally sensuous. When they didn't, they were contraptive and occasionally hallucinogenic. Reading his best work is like riding a dragon's tail down to hell or up to paradise. You never know which it will be. His lesser works, are, well, simply a ride on the tail of a dragon—lots of movement, lots of dragon shit.

Lowry was helplessly attracted to the dragon. He rode his own sentences, and an essential part of him didn't care where they took him. By contrast, James Joyce, who rode a similar dragon, always knew where he was, even if his readers didn't (and don't). Henry James tamed the dragon and made it into a fine riding mare. Samuel Beckett, who understood dragons well and disliked them, wrote his sentences in French and then translated them into English to control the dragon's flight.

All kinds of metaphors to describe Lowry come to mind. He was a language drunk, and a cheap one. He was a classic drunk driver—capricious, irresponsible, self-pitying amid the wreck-age. He didn't mean to run over those poor ideas and objects, he didn't know what he was doing. They're amusing metaphors, but that's all they are. The truth about Lowry is less dramatic.

He was a man who believed that self-control had a physical location, one that was outside himself. He thought it was a *place*. And for most of his life, he sought a sanitorial paradise where his impulse to write and drink could dry out enough for him to gain control over the daemons he believed controlled him. The trouble with that was that he also thought it would be a

---

Naipaul, for instance, is from Trinidad, of East Indian descent. He was raised on that distant Caribbean island, within a Hindu com-munity where cultural traditions were rapidly disintegrating. As soon as he could, he fled Trinidad for England, the logical Imperial Centre for a British colonial, to become a writer—the highest form of existence imaginable. To be a writer, for a colonial, is to live by and within thought itself, and to have the possibility of making a contribution to self-understanding and civil harmony.

Aside from a terror of being without thought, I share several other items of heritage and attitude with Naipaul. I grew up and still live in the Canadian West, which has always had a Third World economy. For many years, being a North American nation of mainly Northern

149

place where he could drink in peace, without hangovers and without remorse. Gabriola Island was to be one of those sanitoriums. One of the last.

It just so happens that for the last ten years I've been spending part of each summer on Gabriola. The island is just off the east coast of Vancouver Island, close to a small city called Nanaimo, which used to be famous for its coal mines but is now famous for its unemployed loggers and its drunks. Both groups get together annually in order to hook outboard motors to the backs of old bathtubs and race the thirty or so miles across the Strait of Georgia to Vancouver. Thousands do it every year. Wealthy drunks come from all over the planet to compete against them. Who needs Kurt Vonnegut to make up things? Nanaimo is as real as your mother.

For me Gabriola Island has been mainly a quiet place to write. I knew Lowry had written about it, and I assumed that because he had, he must have lived there at some point in his life. I had no idea where he'd stayed or how long. At first I didn't much give a damn. But by coincidence, the cabin I rented was among the oldest on the island, and that made me wonder who'd lived in it over the years. For a couple of summers I told myself that my cabin had once been Lowry's, but I let the fantasy idle in neutral. I was there to write, not to read biographies. I was also practising social isolation. For the first few summers I wrote, talked to no one, and didn't waste time trying to confirm the identity of my predecessors.

European descent has masked the nature of our economy from us, but now that is changing as the rich gravy the continent has been stewing in for the last century thins.

If you look carefully, the patterns of industrial and human development here are those of the Third World. The resources are carelessly removed, the profits extracted and removed to distant locations, and those who profit locally eventually flee to more cosmopolitan environments. The natural environment has been exploited brutally, and without serious attempts to regenerate those resources that are renewable.

Now, the middle classes are beginning to split into the familiar hierarchies of those political tyrannies that characterize the upper

But as I grew older and became more interested in collecting materials for writing and less delighted with artistic privacy, I grew more curious about Lowry. I read *October Ferry to Gabriola*. I didn't learn anything specific from that, so I asked several of the local merchants if they knew which of the island's cabins Malcolm Lowry had lived in.

"Who?" they asked.

"Malcolm Lowry. You know."

"Don't recall the name."

"Malcolm Lowry. The writer. You know. Real famous guy."

"Never heard of him. I don't read much myself. Too goddamn busy to read. What kind of stuff did this Lowdry write?"

"Lowry. Malcolm Lowry. English guy. He wrote fiction. Novels."

"Oh yeah," they would say after a moment's uncurious consideration. Then, if they were friendly, they might suggest someone else who might know. Most just grunted and walked away.

No one on the island knew where Lowry had lived. In fact, I couldn't even find anyone who knew who Malcolm Lowry was. No one wanted to know why I was curious about him, come to think of it. Guy comes around the island, drops a few bucks, doesn't talk much, how are they to know he's supposed to be a famous writer? And why should they have been curious? There's only two people on the island who know my name, and I've been around, off and on, for ten years.

Eventually I did find a man who knew about Lowry, and

---

echelons of the Third World: a curiously educated and increasingly poverty-stricken intellectual class, and a wealthy and arrogant upper middle class that has no intellectual interests and prefers to forgo the social and political responsibilities of citizenship for expensive European automobiles, opulent homes loaded with security devices, and a carefully depoliticized personal life circling between resort travel, recreational drugs, personal physical fitness, and exotic cuisine consumed in elegant restaurants. In recent years, it has become increasingly difficult (as it is impossible in the Third World) to be economically well-off, well-informed and liberal at the same time.

The outpost I happened to be raised in was among the last on the continent to get television, and I consider that a crucial piece of luck.

about his stay on the island. At least that's what I thought. His name was Barry Drylis. He's a doctor from Nanaimo. He owns a cabin a few hundred yards down the beach from the one I rent. No, he hadn't ever met Lowry. Barry is about my age, and he doesn't even drink. He just reads a few books now and then.

Barry wasn't clear about exactly where Lowry's cabin was. Someone had told him the name of the road, but he hadn't checked it out in person. Too busy working on his cabin, reading books, or looking into people's throats and ears and noses for that. But I pressed him, and one afternoon he came over to my cabin and told me he'd found the place where Lowry had lived.

"Let's go have a look," I said.

Barry was into physical fitness, so at first he wanted us to ride bicycles to the spot, which he said was about two miles down the coast. I hate riding bicycles, so I talked him out of that plan, and into taking his expensive new Mercedes. He fell for it, but I had to swim back to his cabin with him. Then I had to sit on the hood of the Mercedes while he drove back to my cabin so I could get dry clothing. He wasn't going to let me sit in his new car in my wet bathing suit.

The ride on the hood of Barry's car didn't exactly put me in the best of moods. There was a certain sting to being made into a hood ornament for a guy who specializes in fixing broken noses. And all because of Malcolm Lowry. I lapsed into cynicism: what would we find at Malcolm Lowry's house,

---

It meant that I grew up in essentially the same cultural milieu as most North Americans, but without being subject to its most important interpretive device. Instead of being imprinted by a television screen, I focused on the physical landscape around me. This gave me a self-generated if wildly distorted imagination of the outside world.

I knew it was there, of course. I grew up during the Cold War, believing that the end of the world might start at any second. It was a constant preoccupation, but one for which I had to make up my own images. My imagination was not organized by the banal narrative propaganda of early television nor cluttered by its low-density images of normality. Instead, I dreamed of the shining light of civilization's great centres—the Imperium—my imagination grounded almost solely

anyway? A spiritual redolence? A mountain of mouldering gin bottles?

I was still sulking later when Barry pulled the Mercedes off the main road and onto a cedar-hedged lane that at a casual glance might have been in England. He let the big sedan drift into an alcove and shut off the motor. The transition from windswept Pacific coast to English country lane was an abrupt one, and for a moment I was taken in by it. Lowry must have liked it here, I decided. Then I realized that thirty years ago the hedges wouldn't have been there. They looked nursery-grown, and recently planted.

"Who told you about this," I asked Barry as we climbed out of the car.

He evaded my question. "Nice isn't it? A friend of mine owns it."

"Did he plant the hedges?"

Barry didn't answer. He pushed open the new cedar gate and I followed him into a sheltered garden right out of *Better Homes and Gardens*.

"This is where Malcolm Lowry lived?" I asked, growing more sceptical by the moment.

Barry whirled around with an expansive gesture and pointed to a wooden plaque over the door of the house. "That's what it says."

It wasn't a cabin. It was a house; a very large, new, and expensive house. The plaque over the door read "#1 Malcolm

---

in books, and stimulated by still photography and occasionally, high-density movie images. The Global Village, when it arrived, was seductive, but alien and ultimately opaque. The first wave hadn't arrived in time, and the succeeding waves washed over me without much effect.

From childhood on, I took it for granted that the imaginary world beyond my native environment was something that would have to be *understood*. It was a challenge rather than merely a given. It was mine by heritage, and yet it was not mine, because I could not experience it uncritically. The civil experience I received was similarly disjunctive. It was all cautionary: "watch out for those slicko city bastards", etc. It has made me slightly wary of everything my culture provides.

Lowry Haven''. Beyond it were five more identical rooflines. They were condominiums, and they were brand new.

I walked through the garden and out onto the beach the condos overlooked. Barry followed me, looking just a little sheepish. I glanced back at the roofline again, and saw one more item I hadn't been expecting. On the middle rooftop was a large latticed satellite receiving dish. I wasn't surprised to see it. The dishes were popping up all over the island. Last year the general store on the island scrapped its rack of paperback books and magazines and replaced it with a video cassette rental stall. The proprietors also installed an enormous dish on the store roof, and, according to Barry, were renting movie cassettes they'd taped from the dish.

"This is bullshit, Barry," I said, pointing to the adjoining rooflines. "These are brand new condominiums. Malcolm Lowry never lived here."

He shrugged. "So what?" he said neutrally. "What's wrong with a little redevelopment?"

"I thought you were going to show me where Malcolm Lowry lived. Instead, you show me some fucking tourist resort."

"Hey! This is a tourist island," he said. "All there was here was a couple of dilapidated shacks and a lot of wind. Now people can buy into an authentic piece of local history and enjoy themselves at the same time. I think it's the way to go— capitalizing on the assets we've got."

"I didn't come out here for a lecture on real estate capitalism

---

My equivalent of Naipaul's disenculturated slums are shit-kicking logging camps. His corrupt military dictatorships, for me, are the Chambers of Commerce, the Rotary Clubs. The equivalents are structurally accurate even though they're unorthodox and somewhat imperfect: each environment either interprets or imitates, crudely, the values of a distant Imperium. The chief differences lie in the degrees and kinds of casual violence.

My approach to experience has not changed, and neither has the way I imagine the world, even though I've now seen a fair portion of it in person. For me, as for Naipaul and others with structurally similar backgrounds, experience is less a companion of understanding and more its contrary. In the old colonial world, and in the Third

either, you dork," I said, half under my breath. "Let's go. This is depressing."

Barry wanted to look around, and he was the one with the car. We checked out one of the other "cabins", and sure enough, it also had a plaque over its door: "#2 Malcolm Lowry Haven". Like the other place, it was deserted. I checked out the dish. Like I'd expected, it was hooked into all five units.

While we were driving back I asked Barry who owned the condos.

"Dunno, exactly," he admitted. "They're all from Los Angeles. The one guy I know comes up for a couple of weeks during the summer, then rents it out to college professors during the winter. I think the others do the same. He says it's a hell of a tax write-off."

●

As it happened, Malcolm Lowry Haven was only a few hundred yards from my favorite clam bay. According to the sign nailed onto one of the wind-sculpted trees, the bay was supposed to be contaminated. But the sign was a homemade job, so I figured—correctly—that it was just somebody trying to keep the clams for themselves.

That evening, on an impulse, I drove my rusted-out Japanese stationwagon over to the bay to dig some clams and watch the sun go down. I shovelled out a small bucket of clams and stuck

World, personal experience crushes and demoralizes. It is something that *happens* to the individual and to the collective. It is not a supermarket where one is able to choose and pay for carefully packaged and sterile experiences.

There is one more similarity, and a corollary difference. Like Naipaul, as soon as I reached the age where I could travel independently, I made a pilgrimage to England, our common Imperium. I was enchanted by it, and also terrified, as he has recently admitted that he was. But for a complicated but not very interesting set of reasons—some of which had to do with the existence of attractive alternatives in my homeland, and others which probably had to do with a lack of personal courage—I returned home within a year.

them in the back of the car. I'd brought along a thermos of coffee, and I poured out a cup and sat down on the rocks to enjoy the show. The tide was coming in quickly, and I began to idly scan the margins of the bay. I noticed something in the thick mat of beached seaweed and logging debris the tide was pushing up against the rocks.

I clambered across the rocks and found that the something was the body of a man, lying face down, submerged to the waist in the water. He'd been quite large and stocky, and it looked as if he'd been in his late 40s. The body wasn't bloated, so it hadn't been in the water long. I noticed, almost against my will, how extraordinarily short the arms and legs were, almost to the point of being misshapen. And he wasn't dead, because when I reached him, he groaned.

I turned him over onto his back. His eyes were closed, and his face was bloated enough to have been the face of a drowned man, except that the skin was ruddy, the cheeks starred by broken blood vessels. He seemed oddly familiar.

He opened his eyes and glared at me. "Fuck you, arshhole," he muttered. "Lemme go back to shleep."

Whoever he might be, he was dead drunk. He closed his eyes again and an irregular sigh rattled from his chest. I reached down and shook him. "You're going to drown if you stay here," I said. "Let me give you a hand out of the water."

His eyes opened again. Not a pretty sight. I grabbed his arms and tried to lever him onto his feet. I got him erect, and as I

It is revealing that Naipaul's favorite Conrad story is *An Outpost of Progress* and not *Heart of Darkness*. The narrator of *An Outpost* is detached from the action, and his sentences and his evaluation of the characters and landscapes are short and discursive. They are far from the roiling swirls of *Heart of Darkness* and much of Conrad's other work.

For Naipaul, art comes out of discourse, not the other way around. For him, the medium is not the message because the medium—purely formal art—is the viper of the Imperium. This distrust of art that strays too far from rational discourse and direct evidence is the last colonial attitude that I share with Naipaul. And that, by a somewhat curious route, ties me yet further to Joseph Conrad.

did he took a swing at me, lost his balance and fell backward into the slimy weeds. The water closed around his face, and he came up sputtering and cursing.

The dunking revived him, and he crawled out of the water on his hands and knees. This time I stood back and watched him clamber up onto the dry rocks and sit down. He shook his head to clear the cobwebs.

"Thank you," he said after a moment, gazing at me blearily. His voice was now perfectly lucid, and his accent distinctly British. "I owe you a drink for pulling me out of this."

"I've got a thermos of coffee up on the rocks," I said. "I think that might do you more good."

He grimaced as he stood up and shook himself unsteadily. He looked like a dog that had just come out of the water after fetching a stick. "After you," he said, accepting my offer.

•

"The name's Lowry," he said, as he watched me pour the steaming coffee from the thermos. "Malcolm. Where the hell are we, incidentally?"

"Sure you're Malcolm Lowry," I said, not even trying to stifle my amusement. "I'm Ernest Hemingway, and this is Pilot Bay."

"You've lost weight," he said, obviously prepared to carry on with the gag. "Where is Pilot Bay, might I ask?"

The connection is difficult to explain. Coming as he did from a literate but poor Polish family, Conrad's interpretation of the Imperium of his time was unique. His richly coloured and often windy prose is an astonishing achievement for a non-native speaker, and he was justifiably proud of it. Yet for all that pride, his constant attempts to explain his prose to his readers (the introductions he wrote to his novels are long, obtuse and frequently contradict one another) indicate that he distrusted both that hard-won "style" and the ability of his readers to recognize what he was up to.

His choice of subject matter tells a similar story. Conrad may have written his books from the heart of the Imperium, but he wrote—always—about its boundaries, and about men and women and ideas

"Gabriola Island. You should know that. You're supposed to have lived up on the point over there." "Over where?" he demanded, obviously startled. "Gabriola Island? Are you certain?"

"Sure I'm certain. Who are you? I mean, really."

The man got up without answering and stared across the bay at the point and the line of condominiums. He continued to stare for quite a long time, wavering gently back and forth on the balls of his feet. Then he sat down and gave me a piercing look.

"Jesus Lord Christ in Pandemonium," he said. "How did this happen to me? I must have died and gone to heaven."

"I don't know about that," I said. "I think you got drunk and fell off a boat. Who were you before you became Malcolm Lowry?"

"I've been quite a number of people," he said, quietly. "But when I was drunk, and when I was writing, I was Malcolm Lowry. Every God-forsaken time. And this *is* Gabriola Island."

"Where you lived," I confirmed. "Right over there where those nice dish-connected condos are."

The man stared at me as if I were speaking gibberish. "I didn't live here," he said. "I visited. Once. Stayed less than a day, actually, then went back to Dollarton."

I saw his gaze darting between the condominiums and my car. "That little automobile over there," he said, with a mixture of confusion and awe in his voice. "Is that yours? And that

---

struggling to enter or escape from the Imperial influence.

Naipaul has pointed out a singular quality of Conrad's fiction. "Nothing," he writes, "is rigged in Conrad. He doesn't remake countries. He chose, as we now know, incidents from real life; and he meditated on them." Conrad sought to draw from real events their "aura"—their secret intelligence and truth. The wisdom of the heart, as it was once called.

There is a major problem here. No contemporary writer conscious of his or her position in history (or with an awareness of anatomy and modern surgical advances) can accept Conrad's metaphor of the wise heart. Nor is it possible to believe, with Conrad, that human beings automatically make the leap from image/aura, to understanding and

circular object on the roof of those buildings. What is that? What year is this?"

I decided to humour him. "The year is 1985. 14th of August. That wreck is mine, and the circular object is a satellite receiving dish. What about them?"

"It's a what?"

"It's a device that picks up television signals the American mega-stations bounce off, er, space-craft circling the planet. Offers consumers a choice of up to seventy programs to watch."

"You're serious, aren't you?" he said in a tone that made it clear that he was. "This truly is 1985, and that device works as you say it does?" He swore again, this time more eloquently. "I don't bloody believe it. Do you have a drink?"

"No," I lied. I had a bottle of Scotch back at the cabin, but there was no way I was taking this lunatic anywhere near the place. "Listen, you're Malcolm Lowry and I'm Ernest Hemingway, and theoretically we're both dead as doornails. That being the case, this is probably an illusion that might all go up in a puff of smoke any second. So why don't we sit here while you sober up a little, and we can talk. I've got a few questions I'd like to ask you."

He looked up toward the point again, then back at me. "Okay. I might as well answer your questions. Lord only knows what this is all about."

"What," I said, "can you tell me about the Trojan Horse?"

Lowry laughed. It was an eerie laugh. He let his head sink

---

the action that should be the unavoidable consequence of understanding. Modern science has learned to remove and replace human hearts with machines or with organs taken from dead people. Modern propaganda has managed, on several occasions, to remove the minds of entire nations. The recipient organisms, in both cases, can continue to function, sort of. How can the heart have wisdom or serve as a metaphor when its mysterious sanctity has been so breached, and how can the vaunted intelligence of the public will be trusted?

For all his talk of the wise heart, as a writer Conrad chose, again and again, to interrogate it rather than believe in it. As a mature writer he was no more content to rest within the Imperium than he had been as a young adventurer. He never let himself be lulled by its comforting

back and let himself go into it, like a hyena's hunting giggle. "Let's see. The Trojan Horse. The great dildo of Pallas Athene. I take it you've read Homer.''

"In translation.''

"Ah, m'boy. You must read these things in the original. True beauty is always better in its birthday suit.''

"Stop bullying me with your British education. This is the 1980s. I can't even speak French, and it's an official language in this country.''

"I see you're something of a barbarian.''

"Something,'' I agreed. "Now what about the Trojan Horse?''

"Well,'' Lowry said, both the arch-British accent and the drunken slur vanishing, "being a barbarian you probably want the entire *Ars Poetica* explained to you. So let's begin by saying that the Trojan Horse was a metaphor. One that changed the world.''

"I've already got that far,'' I said, more politely this time. "But it was a metaphor that backfired, wasn't it? After the Trojan War, the Greek tribes collapsed into the isolation of individual self-occupation for nearly four hundred years.''

"Navel-gazing as the Dorian hordes overran them. Yes, I suppose it did backfire in the long run. But it did end the war.''

"Maybe not,'' I said. "The archaeological record indicates that the walls of Troy were probably breached by an earthquake and not by any military action.''

---

systole and diastole. Instead, he traced its arteries to the points of transfer, to the moments of oxygen drop and garbage retrieval. It is the combination of these qualities that makes him a nexus for the contemporary colonial writers.

Things are different now than they were in Conrad's time. The body of the old Imperium has been disembowelled, and its appendages mostly amputated. The nominal unanimity of western culture that reached its apex in the early part of the century—Conrad's time— and which served as the medium of modernism, has been atomized. The circuits of common understanding are down, confined to the cable networks of multiculturalism and political pluralism. We all speak dialects now. We live in divided communes where commoditized

"That's as it may be," Lowry said. "Ancient history is largely conjecture. It's the metaphors it provides that count. So let me tell you about my personal Trojan Horse—the one I fell for, and most of my generation of writers fell for."

"What was that?"

"The novel."

"The novel?"

"Look at it. Any good novel creates a symbolic landscape in which metaphors can create emotions or release trapped ones. People need that. We're all of us far too repressed. A great novel releases great emotions, breaks open the walls of rational consciousness, just as the Trojan Horse broke open the walls of another kind of consciousness."

"Times have changed," I said. "People now have most of their repressed emotions freed. So much so that they run around having emotions about things like laundry detergents and soft drinks. Great, profitable emotions, at least from the perspective of the corporate business sector. It's gotten so that emotion is the least authentic of human behaviours—you never know where the damned things come from. As often as not, they originate in some motivational research laboratory, and you've been fed them as subliminals on television."

Lowry was interested. "One generation's paradise is always the prison of the next. It's the natural result of the insurgence of any culture. But there's no denying what the novel meant for my generation: novelty, oddity of character, emotional

---

private identity is the apotheosis of consciousness, and in which experience has replaced understanding as the goal of thought. The wisdoms of the heart are gone or trivialized; the Imperium has been made invisible. It is, in the most immediate and deepest senses, heartless.

Here is where the division I want to establish resides. For artists comfortable with the Global Village, pluralism, novelty, and formal experimentation is adequate exercise of their faculties. For a colonial, the particulars of physical environment and the tattered rules of discourse are the bases for artistic labour, and for the truth-speaking that is the purpose of art.

Most colonial writers are therefore nervous of invention, particularly

metaphor. Those things were liberating."

"Those are the things that hold my generation hostage," I said. "Even liberation is suspect. You hear about freedom and revolution more often in television commercials than anywhere else."

"Television has become that powerful?" Lowry asked, ruminatively. "Yes, I suppose. It wasn't much in my day, but even then one could see its potential for cheating idiots out of what little native sense they possessed."

"How does the novel become a Trojan Horse?"

Lowry turned his back on me and gazed back at the condominiums and the satellite dish. "Ah. Well, you know what Laocoön said: Beware of Greeks bearing gifts."

"How so?"

He frowned. "Well, the novel was a great gift to humanity. A democratic invention of enormous intellectual force. It provided a sense of individual complexity to a civilization caught up in a class structure—one that wanted to classify people according to who their ancestors were and how much wealth they possessed. Look at Zola and Balzac."

"Let's look at you. All your central characters were cultured drunks who spoke in too-long sentences."

"That's a trifle cruel of you."

"You'll have to excuse me. I've spent my artistic life fighting against the confinements of character, plot, personality, sexuality. Writers of my generation are expected to engage those

---

those inventions that make it their subject matter to tamper with the rules of discourse, or attempt to make Euroamerican syntax, grammar and vocabulary afford the stretchings of meaning that have come to be thought of as style. For a colonial, to puppeteer words or figures is to risk a dangerous ignorance. In Conrad's terms, it is "to create accidents that are properly speaking, accidents only."

To experiment in the manner of the Global Village requires a confidence few colonials can support without uneasiness. And with the ersatz adjacency created by mass telecommunications, the exotic likewise ceases to have any positive meaning. Its inventions too easily become phantoms of psychology and mass political manipulation. The true materials for a colonial are those once-familiar objects and habits

162

things and little else.''

''So?''

''So psychological minutiae and personal quirks aren't the complete constituents of human reality, however fascinating and complicated they may be. If we're going to continue on this planet, we have to find ways to register a more synchronic and detailed kind of intellectual and artistic attention. For the last thirty years there have been bombers flying over our heads twenty-four hours a day, each plane loaded to capacity with nuclear weapons, and a certain percentage never more than a few minutes to failsafe. And I'm expected to confine my artistic investigations to how people feel about their bodies or their disappointments over not getting a better job. The causalities open to examination are self-enclosing—our mothers forgot to clip our fingernails when we were children and now we suffer from an impulse to scratch our lovers while having sex. That sort of thing. I'm bored to shit with the daemonic. The novel has become part of the conspiracy of lies and irrelevance that is using up the planet and threatening daily to turn us all into a heap of radioactive debris.''

''I see,'' Lowry said, quietly.

''No you don't. Right now, you're peeking up the beach toward those condominiums wondering if someone might be willing to serve you a martini. This is an important story here, to me at least, and I'd appreciate it if you'd damned well pay attention.''

---

of communal life.

As a First World colonial, my position is nearly as peculiar as Conrad's was in 1890. My response is the logical one: to repress all taste for adventure, both as a citizen and as an artist. I do it deliberately, and at times perversely. The true adventure can only be here, in the throat of the behemoth, close to its brain and its centre of articulation. There is no reason to crawl down to its tail just to feel its massive weight on me. Yet even while I can say all this with conviction, I am haunted by Cambodia, by the Congo, and by the ghost of Joseph Conrad.

"Let me turn this back on you," Lowry said, gently. "What's *your* metaphor? How would you want the novel to operate?"

"My metaphor is either the Global Village—or its progenitor, the Trojan Horse. I'm trying to see the one through the other. You don't know anything about the Global Village, so it isn't your problem. Be thankful for that. I'd explain it, but it's opaque because of the commercial rhetoric it's loaded with, sort of like a computer with a thatched straw cover on it. And it's assiduously kept from close scrutiny. That dish over there is one of its few coherent symbols."

"Go on," he said.

"Not here," I answered. "There's not enough time. But maybe I can explain the Trojan Horse in a more helpful way. We've more or less agreed that it wasn't, in essense, a physical contraption representing a horse. It's more than that, a new intellectual tool that appeared to free humanity, but in fact did the opposite. It created the prison of rational consciousness. In a minor way, the novel is the same thing, and for that reason I don't want it to operate at all. I want it dead, buried and forgotten—Freud-stained sailor suit and all."

"Ah, you can't mean that, about the novel."

"Why not? It's now a dangerous form of expression, at least given the limitations you accepted for it. More important, it's no longer an adequate form of human experience. It takes the writer out of his or her moral imagination—mostly these days into sociometric manipulations, and it takes the reader out of

---

9

Haunted by the ghost of Joseph Conrad? He's a great writer, a messenger. Instead of being haunted by him, I should be stealing him blind, picking the pockets of the ghost. After all, that's why Hermes, the messenger of the Greek gods, was the protector of thieves and poets. Stealing from the writers of the past is part of a writer's basic repertoire.

I'm haunted because at the same time as I want to claim Conrad, I can't figure out what to steal from him, or how to do it. His work was never conventional literature, however hard he tried to make it so during his lifetime. That he did not succeed is part of the reason

the social and intellectual structures that lead to change."

"It doesn't have to," Lowry said.

"That's like saying that nuclear physics doesn't have to lead to nuclear weapons. But it has, and now there are about 20,000 nuclear warheads kicking around the planet, enough to vaporize us all a thousand times over. Any productive force decays to its most venal possible use when a market economy overpowers both its cultural and political institutions as it has done here. Imagination decays too, unless it builds in safeguards against that decay."

"How is that done?"

"I don't know," I admitted. "I hoped you might."

Lowry moved off the rock he'd been perched on, and slipped down, crab fashion, several rocks closer to the water. "You might, ah, try to stay in the interzones," he said, slowly, as if he were dragging the reluctant thoughts out of himself as he spoke. "I always tried to write my way out of them—into hell, or into a paradise. But I lived in the interzones—in Dollarton I was literally atop the primeval ooze. I think that's why I was drawn back time and again. And I wrote from that vantage point, always."

"Why did you stay there?" I asked, feeling less aggressive now. "In Dollarton, I mean. And outside England."

"I'm not sure," he said unsteadily. "There were reasons, of course. Family upbringing, the Imperial crush. I had cultural claustrophobia. But I had deeper instincts, you know. Strange

---

for his work's contemporary importance. It is both more and less than conventional literature, just as Conrad himself was more and less than a conventional writer. As Naipaul points out, everything he wrote is a singular man's informed meditations upon a geographical location and the effects that location had on the displaced persons, native or exotic, who attempt to inhabit it.

There are at least two items in this that are worth noting. First, his stories, which are grounded firmly in historical verities and personal experience, are never self-expressive. The other item may partially explain the first one: at some point in almost everything he wrote, there is the possibility of collapse. Chaos is never far away, either from his characters or from the sentences he writes.

ones, that told me to live in the interzones between the worn out Cartesian universe and the wilderness. Gabriola Island was to be one of them, but it didn't work out. I have an uneasy soul, or something akin to one. And remember, I was a Christian. I was looking for mercy, expiation, paradise. I wasn't looking for social change.''

Lowry laughed his hyena laugh, but this time it was almost pleasant. "So now you find me here, like the Orpheus head, and all the prophesy I can offer you is to tell you to go on doing what you're doing—beachcombing. What a world!''

I lay back on the rocks, and gave in to the soft night breezes moving off the uplands. In the dusky light I could feel the rocks giving up their stored heat. Above me there were stars, the familiar summer constellations beginning their evening traverse of the heavens. One of the stars was moving: a satellite. On a reflex, I glanced back at the dish. Yeah, I thought. What a world. Behind me I heard a cough, soft and apologetic, like an elderly man clearing his throat. I turned in the direction of the cough, but it was no old man. A cougar stood behind us, no more than a few yards away. I moved, slowly, slowly, until was able to prod Lowry with my outstretched foot. He turned toward me, and when he saw the cougar, he smiled.

As if the animal knew him, it padded across the rocks past me and lay down beside him, in an heraldic pose.

"This is what the metaphor gives us," he said, stroking the cougar's tawny back. "We still have this.''

Absent from Conrad's novels and stories are the over-confident conventionalities that, for instance, make Stephen King's positionings of normal people against abnormal reality so easily digestible and unthreatening, and they are without the faith in an invisibly creative taxonomy of language that makes the prose of James Joyce so, er, fascinating.

Conrad's life and writing constitute a curiously revealing transposition of the life and writing of Arthur Rimbaud, the quintessential artist of the Imperium. Rimbaud was so arrogantly confident of the stability of European civilization that he was willing to turn it upside-down, spit in its face, and then take its bright entrepreneurial spirit to Africa. Rimbaud's confidence eventually cost him his health and his life, but

Starship

It started a couple of months back, right around Christmas. My wife bought me a copy of *People* magazine so I'd have something to read while the kids fooled around with their presents. In the magazine there was a feature article on hot new public figures, and among the so-called rising political stars, there he was. President Kennedy's son. John, I think his name is. He's about to go into politics, running for some sort of state office. Nice looking kid, and probably smart as hell, just like his father was. The article didn't say anything about him wanting to be president, but that hardly matters. He's a Kennedy, and they're going to kill him just like they killed his father and his uncle.

I didn't figure it out right then, of course. Look, I don't claim to be able to predict the future. I just happen to be able to add two and two together and come up with four. I might not have even tuned into the whole thing if one of the photographs of the Kennedy kid hadn't got stuck in my head. There was something strange about it, you know? Something not quite right. The background was too fuzzy, like it was a telephoto

---

one senses that for Rimbaud, personality didn't quite matter. He knew that French Literature would lay his darling bones to rest in its eternally lighted palaces.

By contrast, Conrad was never quite confident of anything he had to do, either as a man or as a writer. As a private man he treated all human beings, as Ford Madox Ford was noted, with an almost oriental deference and humility, as if by their very existence each human being he encountered were honouring him. But as a writer, he wrote sentences that are alternately drafty and suffocatingly close, his critical pronouncements alternately brilliant and biliously ultimate. He wrote as if he feared the whole shadow play might collapse around him before he could get it right. For him, literature was an excruciatingly bright

shot, and he looked so innocent, so intent on what he was doing. It was no posed photo. You could tell that the young Kennedy didn't know he was being photographed.

It put me off-kilter most of Christmas day, at least until my wife lost her temper and yelled at me for lousing up the big day for the kids. Anyway, I put it on the back burner and carved the turkey and sang Christmas carols just like we always do. But in bed that night I got to thinking again.

When the first one, John F. was killed, I was only seventeen. It felt like the unthinkable had happened. In a funny way, after that, anything and everything became thinkable and possible. By the time Bobby Kennedy was killed, it had changed, what with the war in Vietnam and the way all the peace and love stuff was going all to hell and getting commercialized. What had become possible and thinkable with the first killing had now become inevitable. I remember when Bobby was down talking to Cesar Chavez and the farm workers a few weeks before it happened. I thought then that he looked like a man who was marked for killing. I mean, he was showing us that he could grow and change and be a hell of a lot more open than anyone had ever imagined a president could be. And he was saying that the government could be like that too. I still believe that if he'd made it, governments would have changed, everywhere. They'd all have changed because nobody would have stood for it if they hadn't.

When Bobby Kennedy was assassinated, something in me died

---

and beautiful illusion.

He was right, as writers are now finding out. But that is only part of the point I want to make here. For Conrad, as for all colonial writers, language was merely a medium to carry the messages he was never sure of until the labour of transforming experience and thought into understanding had been completed.

Bingo! In the Global Village—the immaterial new Imperium—there is no public art, and therefore no messages that are widely transmitted. Thought, which for colonial artists is everything, has now been relegated a minor role in the artistic formula, its applications either academic or vulgar. It is a secondary commodity, useful chiefly as a personal subjunct to the acquisition of the primary commodity,

with him. I mean, I'm not even an American, just a guy living in a neighbouring country with the same military and political fate, part of this Global Village business.

I kind of gave up after that. I realized that good people couldn't make the world change, and I let the world start changing me. I was going to university then, and I quit about a month after the assassination. I came back here and applied for a job at the smelter.

I've done okay, so I'm not complaining about my own life. The wife and I get along pretty well, and the kids are great. I'm a shift foreman now, the mortgage is coming down, and thank God all of us have got pretty good health.

But that photograph from *People* magazine stayed with me right through Christmas. And after. It got stuck in the Grey Zone, sort of. I thought I'd forgotten about it, but it was there, right beneath the surface. When the Space Shuttle exploded, it bubbled right up and over the top. That's when I began to put it together, the two and two.

I was home that day. I work split-shift, and it was my day off. I was having lunch when the announcement came over the radio. I stopped eating and walked into the living room and flicked on the television. I didn't move for at least two hours.

The first thing I saw was the explosion, twice in succession. At that point they didn't know exactly what had happened. They weren't even sure that the astronauts were dead, although it seemed pretty clear to me that nothing could have survived that

---

which is consumer experience. Life in the Global Village is not meant to be understood and it is not meant to be interpreted. It is only meant to be experienced. And even then the experiential medium is not life but the Global Village itself.

As a colonial, my instinct is that any village—even the Global Village—must have location and boundaries, despite a rational acknowledgement that the Global Village by definition is locationless and omniscient. I have witnessed its effect on my kin, those who are by birth and geography the logical and announced recipients of the Global Village's benefits.

I'm talking about people who live in towns and cities too small to support the illusion that they are cosmopolitan. For them, the Global

kind of explosion. For some reason I'm not sure about, I started counting the number of times they showed the Shuttle explode. In two hours I saw it twenty-two times. Gruesome.

I was fascinated. Who wasn't? But the longer I watched, the more I started seeing things I don't think I was supposed to see. It was like I was looking *through* the television set, and seeing how the television system was shaping the story, connecting it to parts of the public psyche and disconnecting it from others, turning it into something it wasn't in the beginning. A lot of the details were pretty cruel, like when they filmed the high school the teacher on board taught at, and we had to watch the glee of the kids turn into shock and horror. Or when they showed the expressions on the faces of the astronauts' families as *they* watched the Shuttle go up and then explode. It was weird the way the cameras were running around violating those poor people. And what for? So all of us on the business end of television could experience the explosion in new ways. Why the hell did they do that?

I kept thinking, *I just watched seven human beings die.* That got me thinking about a few other things. They kept repeating the same set of facts. Mostly it seemed to have something to do with the shortness of the flight. The Shuttle had been in the air for sixty-seven seconds or something like that, when it exploded. For sixty-seven seconds those seven astronauts thought they were headed for a great big adventure. I wondered what they thought in the split second they had to realize that

---

Village exists in the sky. Their satellite dishes point upward, suppliant, to receive its manna. There are a hundred more dishes every day.

But the manna doesn't nourish my people. Instead, it diminishes and humiliates them, by presenting images of impossibly finished and stylish landscapes; images of men who are virile, well-dressed, urbane and violent; women who are beautiful, sexually alluring, remote in their polished perfections. They are the perfect consumers of product, these television perfections; unhampered by inability, unwillingness, or second thoughts, serenely thoughtless in their slickly violent confrontations with ugliness and the other human frailties they treat as evil.

My would-be Global Villagers ingest these images happily. But

their big adventure was over, and so were their lives. I began wondering what people think about when they're dying. I guess I wondered and thought about a lot of strange things in those two hours. Things I hadn't thought much about for years.

I even thought about the fact that at least seven people must have died of starvation somewhere in the world during those sixty-seven seconds, and that nobody gave a damn about them because their deaths weren't spectacular. They just stopped breathing, and their hearts stopped beating. No big deal. I hadn't thought that way since University, when everybody was thinking about things like that. I even thought about why nobody cares about those kinds of deaths the way they used to. I got an ugly answer back: *because there are no television cameras there to film the dying.*

Like I said, I didn't move for two hours. I kept watching until they started showing commercials again. When the commercials came back on, I got up and walked down to the store for some smokes and a six-pack of Coke. When I got back, though, I plunked myself right back down in front of the television. I stayed there when the kids got home from school. We had dinner in the living room that night.

It was late in the afternoon when they started showing the person-in-the-street interviews. And there it was, in one of the first interviews. Some woman in Ohio said something about how there hadn't been a tragedy like this since the Kennedys were killed. And right after the interview a commentator came on

---

eventually they click off their television sets, and must face themselves and their environment. They gaze at one another, men, women and children, and see the ugliness, the lack of grace, the absence of camera make-up, the genetic imperfection of their own pitted faces, their bodies spavined by heavy labour. In disgust they abandon self and home. But there is nowhere to go. There are only trailer parks, shacks, prefabricated buildings designed three thousand miles away and trucked in from factories five hundred miles distant. There are littered, unpaved roads; abandoned cars; parts from worn-out machines. They can experience the Global Village only through its distant media images, and through the endless flow of its consumer commodities. The television sets are turned on again, and they gravitate to them

and brought it up again. It was like the killings of the Kennedys, he said. A World Tragedy.

That really got me upset. The Shuttle blowing up was unfortunate all right, but it wasn't like the assassinations of the Kennedys. When the Kennedys died, something more than a Kennedy ceased to breathe. Like I said. Something essential and good disappeared, and something selfish and cold-blooded and evil took its place. Something good died in a lot of people that day. I know something in me died. And it was so dead I forgot about it for years and years.

Let me get this straight. I remember when they shot Bobby, I felt sadness, and maybe I got depressed in a more or less clinical way. I think a lot of people felt sad, but for me there was something else there too, something about halfway between feeling hopeless and feeling helpless. I remember saying to myself a few hours after Bobby was declared dead, and I'd seen the shooting four or five times on television: *They kill the Kennedys because the Kennedys die so beautifully.*

So there I am, eighteen years later, watching the television and trying to imagine the seven astronauts and trying to put their deaths together with the Kennedy killings. And meanwhile I'm getting bombarded, again and again, with the film footage of the explosion. I saw the Space Shuttle explode fifty-two times in the next two days. I saw it in slow motion, in freeze frame, and as the hours passed, I saw it from new angles. I even saw it as a cartoon, for Christ sake. In forty-eight hours I probably

---

greedily. Why not? Their own lives and landscapes are visibly inferior.

It doesn't interest them that Global Village commodities are expensive in the outposts, loaded with freight costs and hidden taxes, and frequently useless or inappropriate. Nor does it help to shout that the induced craving for them, seeded by subliminals, guts the value of what is local and authentic. Indigenous materials are inferior. If they weren't, someone would make a franchised operation out of them, right? Even indigenous craft, and the skills associated with it, are now given the humiliating designation of "folk art".

And so Mickey Mouse and Ronald McDonald replace traditional or local heroes in every child's imagination while the local franchises carry off the profits to head offices in the new Imperium.

saw it as many times as I've seen John and Bobby Kennedy die over the years.

But what made all the pieces come together wasn't the footage of the Shuttle. It was something on the eleven o'clock news the day of the explosion. It was clip about two minutes long, casual as hell, about Bobby Kennedy's eldest son. Not the one who's already dead, and I don't think its the one who lost his leg from cancer. No, that one is Ted Kennedy's son.

I'd never seen this Kennedy before. The story was about how he's planning to run for some local office in Massachusetts. And the film had that same fuzzy quality to it that the article in *People* magazine on young John Kennedy had—like they were photographing something that happened a long time ago, when the world was a different kind of place than it is now—like, warmer and better and one hell of a lot sweeter.

I didn't get much sleep that night. First thing the next morning I turned the house upside-down looking for the issue of *People* that had John Kennedy Jr. in it. I found it, and the minute I looked at the photograph of Kennedy I knew what it was that'd upset me the night before when I'd seen the film of Bobby Kennedy's kid: *the cameras had cross-hairs on their lenses*, as if they were the scope of a sniper's rifle.

The harder I stared at the *People* magazine photo the easier it got to see. I showed the photo to my wife, but she couldn't see the cross-hairs at all. I said to hell with her, and got on the phone. When I couldn't get through to anyone, I pulled out

---

What is happening to us? We are, after all, *Homo Sapien*—thinking man. Thought (and I say this with careful neutrality, recognizing the possible ironies) is what got us here. Yet who can deny that the goal of Global Village mass communications technology is to transform the complexities of contemporary life into a reality that resembles the Saturday morning cartoons? It is as if free consciousness itself has been recognized as the worm in the apple, and the Disneyfied platonists of the Global Village are intent on returning us to Eden. They are planning to do it by humiliating consciousness and destroying memory.

That's what the Khmer Rouge—admittedly by much more crude and violent methods—also attempted to do. They wanted a world in

the typewriter and started in on the letters. I wrote them to everyone I could think of. I wrote to the Networks, telling them what I knew, and I wrote to the newspapers. I even wrote one to Ted Kennedy, warning him to get all those kids the hell out of there. And in between I watched the coverage of the Space Shuttle explosion whenever it came on.

I've been just a little nuts ever since. It's been eighteen years since the lights went out for Bobby Kennedy. But now they're on again for me. I know who killed the Kennedys. Not in the conventional sense. I mean, we'll never really know who it was that killed John Kennedy. Lee Harvey Oswald or whoever helped him don't count. And sure, Sirhan Sirhan pulled the trigger on Bobby. But I know *what* and *who* got them to do it. Television made them do it. Television put the cross-hairs over their beauty.

Sure it sounds loony. Maybe it is. But so are a lot of things. I'm pretty sure I'm not the only one who's figured this one out. I don't know what I'll do about it, but I'm sure of one thing. I'm not going to let them kill these new Kennedy boys. Maybe I'll have to stand in front of them when the shooting starts. Okay. If I have to I will. That's a promise.

---

which people existed without memory and without the ability or will to think independently. They tried to replace those uniquely human abilities with direct experience framed by an absolute and monadic authority. It is also what Conrad's Kurtz wanted to bring to the Congo natives in the 1890s.

Sure, the Imperial impulse has changed. And it has not changed at all. Almost a century has passed since Conrad travelled into the heart of the Congo. Now that immaterial heart seems to be everywhere.

10

Let's go over some of this. What have I discovered that I didn't know

The Swan and Leda

I have a lot of respect for William Butler Yeats, but I've got
to tell you his famous poem "Leda and the Swan" isn't accurate.
The alleged rape of Leda didn't happen the way he described
it. It was a very different kind of event. Swans do not rape.
They don't have to. And only those who have gazed into the
eyes of a swan will truly understand why.

Relax. I'm not writing this from jail. I haven't had sex with
a swan. But I have met one, and I have looked into its eyes.
In quite a non-mystical way, I have communed with the swan,
and it has given me an insight into the real story of Leda and
Zeus and all the history that followed from their encounter.

"Take me home with you," the swan whispered.

It didn't say why it wanted me to take it home. There was
a delicious moment in which our eyes were locked.

"I don't even know if you're male or female," I said without
thinking.

"Who cares?" said the swan.

"I can't take you home," I said, tearing my gaze from the

---

when I started? One thing I'm certain of is that what happened in
Cambodia after 1975 was not irrational or spontaneous, however
deeply it horrifies our sensibilities. Horror isn't going to keep it from
happening again. There is a causality to the Khmer Rouge atrocities—
not a strict or absolute one, but one more nearly absolute than random.

What did the Americans do to make it happen? Between 1969 and
1973 U.S. military aircraft dropped 539,000 tons of bombs into the
Cambodian countryside—nowhere near the amount dropped on Vietnam and slightly less than were dropped on Laos, but more than the
Allies dropped on Germany during World War II. The bombings of
Cambodia are said to have resulted in half a million deaths, and they
are said to have destroyed 80 percent of the rice fields and killed 75

175

swan's and trying to sound more firm than I felt. "I'm a human being, and you're a swan. You don't belong in my world."

I thought about my two cats, one of which is inordinately fond of birds. Recently it had coldcocked an unsuspecting seagull that happened to land within his small but extremely immediate sphere of attention. The cat pounced on it, knocked it senseless, and was proudly dragging his very large acquisition into the house through an open window when the gull regained consciousness. The ensuing melee left the place in a shambles. I also have a part-labrador pup who shows a certain genetically-based interest in chasing birds of any kind. My house is no place for a sweet-eyed bird.

"I love you," the swan cooed, interrupting my unspoken run of excuses.

"Aw, come on," I chided. "You love everybody. I can see it in your eyes. And if it makes you feel better, I like you too. A lot. But I can't take you home with me."

"How about something to eat, then," the swan countered reproachfully.

I rummaged through my pockets, instantly feeling guilty. "I brought a bag of birdseed," I said apologetically, "but my kids fed it to the ducks. All I've got now is some chips."

The swan cocked its head without taking its eyes off me. "What flavour are they?" it cooed, shuffling a little closer to the fence.

"Taco."

---

percent of the draft animals.

Those figures are approximate. They may underestimate the numbers. More probably they exaggerate them. But I've learned that one should be wary of statistics, for two reasons. First, the relationship they have with truth is primarily conceptual. Second, statistics are frequently statements of the prejudices of those who assemble them, as "factual" reality always is.

The more statistics on Cambodia I've encountered, the more sceptical I've become. One analyst, to give you an example, translated the 539,000 *tons* of bombs into *pounds* to inflate the impact of the statistics. That way, it came out to slightly more than a billion pounds. The zeros are convincing, but that kind of emotionalization is

"Shit. I despise taco flavoured chips. They upset my stomach. I only like the plain ones."

"I'm sorry," I mumbled. "They tasted fine to me."

The swan looked away, as if unable to bear the disappointment. Then it turned back to me.

"Will you come back next week?" it asked, looking straight into my eyes once again. "Please?"

I felt like a chicken trying to avoid the hypnotic gaze of a cobra. Well, no, it wasn't quite that bad. I *tried* to feel like I was being manipulated. No luck.

I glanced over at my two sons. They were staring at me suspiciously. Their father was having a conversation with a large bird, which was, after all, something they had not encountered on television except maybe on *Sesame Street*. And they know that the bird on that program is really only a man dressed up to look something like a bird. In their eyes, my behaviour was inappropriate, and maybe weird. I felt a small swirl of resentment toward them, not so much because they disapproved of the swan and me, but because they'd wasted the entire bag of birdseed getting some stupid ducks to follow them around as if they were Pied Pipers. And now, the little egomaniacs were deciding that I was crazy.

"Bring me some sardines," the swan whispered, bending its neck and poking its soft head through the wire fence into my hand. "King Oscar. They're so much better than the cheaper brands."

---

dangerous. After he translated tons into pounds he made a factual error based on his own inflation of the statistic, claiming that more bombs had been dropped on Cambodia than were used by all belligerents in World War II.

Some of the errors made in pursuit of scholarly accuracy were even more damaging. Michael Vickery, who, along with Ben Kiernan, has been perhaps the best informed and careful of Khmer Rouge Cambodia's analysts, has introduced an attractive concept he calls the "Standard Total View", the ironic acronym of which is "STV". STVs are those simplified combinations of dramatic images and often barely interpreted statistics and facts presented to us daily by the international news media about what is going on in the world. The STV of

"You do this to lots of people," I said to the swan. "Don't you?"

"No," the swan answered quietly. There was a hint of irony in its voice. "You're the very first."

I haven't gone back. I have a complicated life as it is, and I know that if I were to go back I might do anything the swan asked, and that in a very short time my life would be ruined, cats, dogs, kids and all. And anyway, literature is full of those kinds of stories, even if life doesn't seem to be anymore.

•

Let's go back to Mr. Yeats. Some parts of his poem are correct. He was correct in thinking that swans are capable of having sexual intercourse with human beings. Most birds can't, including eagles, ravens, condors and vultures. Ostriches can, but it doesn't seem to happen very often. Only a select few birds have the right equipment, and swans are atop the list. The rest of the birds on the planet make do with an all-purpose cloaca, and when they mate, it is aerial, instantaneous, a brief bum-bump in the bright air. I've known a few people—mostly women, actually—who complain about their men in roughly the same terms, but for most of us, sexual experience is a little more complicated, and, er, deeper and longer.

Second, I can't see any reason to doubt that Zeus did conceive a passion of sorts for the beautiful Leda, but there is reason

---

Cambodia holds that the Khmer Rouge were wholly evil, and that they perpetrated an absolute reign of irrational terror and brutality across Cambodia for the duration of the regime. As an academic, Vickery naturally finds the STV abhorrent.

He points to evidence—good evidence—that the Khmer Rouge probably didn't kill 40 per cent of the population, or even 25 per cent. Quite probably they only killed 15 or 20 per cent—something just over a million human beings, instead of the two or three million estimated elsewhere. Likewise, he points out that the distribution of brutality wasn't absolute, citing evidence that during 1975-76, no more than 5,000 to 10,000 were executed in the Eastern Zone, and then only for resisting the authority of the cadres. It was only in 1977 and

to question the nature of that passion as depicted by Yeats and by some of the old myths. In the cosmology of the Greeks, the gods, unlike human beings, rarely had only one thing in mind, and Zeus, who was the chief god, always had an ulterior motive—usually an educative one.

The Greeks (who after all invented Zeus) needed to put an end to the powerful city of Troy because it sat directly in the path of all the best trade routes to Asia Minor. Leda was the medium and the opportunity for producing precisely the right mix of human passions and abilities that would lead to Troy's destruction. So, into the body of the swan Zeus leaped, metaphorically speaking. An indeterminate time later, Leda, presumably also metaphorically, is said to have laid one or two or four eggs, depending on whose version of the story you accept as the correct one.

We could reduce the tale to a boring discussion of the nature of metaphor or of local politics if we pursue this line of explanation much further. And we'd be missing the point—and the fun. So let's get back to Yeats and his telling of the tale. It is in his depiction of the coupling of god and woman that Mr. Yeats loses control of his materials. We can accept, for the sake of the tale, that Zeus conceived a divine passion for Leda. No problem. But the other side of the Yeats story is all wrong.

I figure Leda must have fallen for a swan, possibly in much the same way I fell for mine. For months, every weekend, she went to the bird sanctuary just outside Sparta with the equivalent

---

1978 that the bloodbath got underway, and then at the hands of the cadre from the Centre area—Pol Pot's supporters.

Somehow, finding out that the Khmer Rouge were only two-thirds as brutal as depicted by the STV, or that there were some relatively humane people among the Khmer Rouge authorities, isn't very comforting. The STV of Cambodia may be factually untrue, but the scholarly search for factuality in a situation that is beyond fact and statistics must likewise be distrusted. One is tempted to say that only in the academic world is there such a thing as a "relative atrocity". The truth is less sanguine. Most major governments in the twentieth century have perpetrated "relative atrocities", occasionally in the interest of civil order. All are capable of it.

of the King Oscar sardines my swan asked me for. Zeus must have spotted her at the bird sanctuary—he was a well-known bird-watcher—and merely hopped inside her chosen swan to take advantage of the attraction that was already in full bloom.

Their union couldn't have been a brutal one. There was almost certainly a tentativeness in it, a sweetness, soft billings and cooings. Thighs and feathers stroked alike. Probably there was a quiet discussion of the anatomical awkwardnesses, and during and after their lovemaking, a great deal of tenderness. And if, at the moment of orgasm, the swan lifted his great wings, spread them across Leda's thighs and let loose a cry of ecstasy, well, what of it? Leda was probably vocalizing at the same time. I'm willing to bet big bucks that most people have heard or made noises—screams, groans and grunts—of less aesthetically pleasing quality, and a few (not me, of course) have even made invocations to a deity. Maybe it was an invocation from Leda that gave the locals the idea that she was getting it on with an important god.

Yeats raises the question of whether or not, in the midst of her ecstasy, Leda understood the divine intentions within her swan. Translated, he was asking if she saw how the sensible but quite business-like political intelligence of Greece was going to destroy the threat of Troy, and how, having done so, it would deal with the megalomania of its victorious forces.

On a slightly different track, it is revealing that the Greeks have argued bitterly over every aspect of this story except the

---

Such errors weren't dishonest ones, but the examples hold. The more exact the numbers given are, the more reality slippage there is likely to be. Most of the Cambodia statistics are either crude estimates, or they are distortingly partisan. And anyway, it is much more important to ask questions like: why did the American military bomb a neutral country with such indiscriminate fury?

That question has never been answered adequately. There are explanations, of course. The strategic explanations we know about: disrupt the Ho Chi Minh Trail, kill Viet Cong, capture or kill the PRG and the NLF. But beyond that, the explanations start to get weird.

reality and purpose of Leda's coupling with the swan. Some, for instance, said that only Helen of Troy was born of the union, and that the other three children born at the same time were merely mortal and relatively unfated. Others argued for different combinations of mortality and divinity, egg or live birth.

None of them seemed to have thought it unusual that Leda had sexual intercourse that same night with her husband Tyndareüs, and no one mentioned that in her supposedly bruised and violated condition, the husband noted nothing untoward about her appearance and demeanour. And, notwithstanding the renowned sensitivity of modern Greek males, you should be convinced by that fact alone that no act of violence took place with the swan.

One of the other offspring of that steamy afternoon tryst in ancient Greece, became, in her way, as famous as Helen. This was Helen's sister, Clytemnestra. She and Helen married brothers, and it was Clytemnestra who married the more powerful of the two. She married Agamemnon, who was the High King of all the Mycenaean tribes, and was the commander of the Greek force that attacked Troy after Paris "kidnapped" Helen. Clytemnestra believed that her husband sacrificed one of their daughters in order to get the Greek fleet to Ilium. And when, ten years later, Agamemnon returned in overweening triumph, and with a dozen or so docile Trojan concubines in his luggage, his wife and her lover murdered him before he had time to sit down in his own living room. This set off another

---

The U.S. had a surplus of explosives, equipment and pilots, and an overheated military/industrial complex pushing the government for contracts. Alvin Toffler or Noam Chomsky would like that explanation. Cambodia, with its ancient erotic civilization buried in the jungle of lianas, and with its wild tribesmen, frightened Americans in ways that North Vietnam's courageous Russian-backed Marxist-Leninists never did. Americans understand courage, and they think they understand Russian foreign policy. But the sensuous Cambodian jungles defied understanding. Now we're hearing from Norman Mailer and the critic/worshippers of Phallocracy.

I think the motives for the bombing of Cambodia had the same disturbed logic as Conrad's French man-of-war shelling the Congo

series of events, the Oresteia, and that set off another, and so on and so forth, until you find yourself wondering why you don't get along easily with your family, and I find myself wondering how long it would take to nip on out to the bird refuge.

•

Stories like that sort of make life sound reasonable and grand and connected, don't they? The Greek message is always the same: Life resonates, and we are inevitably, unalterably part of those resonances if we look and listen carefully enough.

One of the things I like about myth is that it just isn't a commercial medium. When we talk in mythic terms, no matter what we do, no matter the numbers of Hostess Twinkies that sulk, half digested, in our intestines, we are within a continuum of events that links us in a common narrative, a story which is at once personal and common to all. Sure, the action these days is often fouled by commercials, and most of us fall asleep in the parts where the story doesn't seem to be about us, but that's because we've been conned into thinking the complexities of existence are voluntary; that in a democracy, participation is optional.

You're not sure what I'm talking about? Well, as I write this, there is a woman walking along the street toward the cafe I'm sitting in. She is a slight woman, stoop-shouldered, perhaps thirty years old. She walks with the staggering gait of someone

---

jungle in 1890. Maybe that's the trick. All explanations of Cambodia are first and finally exercises in logic.

The craziest people in the world are logical. Governments have become even more logical. They enact the twisted assumptions behind their logic, and that's all. Ultimate questions are neither asked nor answered, and none need to be in the seductive passage of a logical process. The confirmation of logic merely requires capitulation to limited assumptions and the elimination of contrary phenomena. In this world, logic is generally a tool for avoiding ultimate questions.

Then there's the Khmer Rouge. Also, finally, questions without answers; explanations that are more speculation than fact. It's partially accurate to say that the Khmer Rouge were a creation of the trauma

who is recurrently and chronically afraid, and thus attempts to see in all dark directions at once. Both her eyes are blackened from some sort of beating. But unaccountably she is grinning, almost idiotically. Perhaps she is ironically chiding herself for having walked into a door. Perhaps she is on her way to a centre for battered women. On the bright side, perhaps she has just landed a hatchet in the forehead of her slope-headed husband, or she's seen her favourite heroine on the afternoon television soap operas similarly dispatch a tormentor. More depressingly, perhaps she's merely bombed on the tranquillizers her family doctor has given her in order to help her 'adjust' to her domestic difficulties. And perhaps, she has just made love with a swan. Perhaps, perhaps; the possibilities are almost infinite. And all of them are connected.

This isn't *quite* the way the Greeks would have seen it, nor is it the world according to W.B. Yeats. Writing more than a half-century ago, Yeats still believed that a reasonable and grand and connected order was at the heart of human existence—a cosmology, to use the vernacular. For him, Zeus was the personification of all that, a benign magnificence that drew some of the animal violence out of the planet by means of a grand scheme to defuse brute chaos and then to give it structure. All else that was good, for Yeats, followed from that impulse toward order.

The Greeks didn't try to create so absolute an order by their speculations and tales. Instead, they observed, they talked, and

---

and social disruption of the bombing of Cambodia, a reactive movement with minimal ideological and organizational structure, inexperienced in everything except brutality, destruction and death. But the peculiar character of the Khmer Rouge has deeper and more complex roots. Recent Khmer Rouge history is filled with brutal Issarak bandits and anti-Vietnamese isolationism. The urban/rural hostilities apparent in the Khmer Rouge era can be tracked still further into the country's political and religious past. Similarly, one must not forget that the Khmer Rouge were nurtured by Maoist China during its most crazed period, and that China certainly encouraged long-standing Khmer hostilities towards the pro-Soviet North Vietnamese. Circumstances also played a powerful role. The Khmer Rouge were

they cherished the multiplicity and apparent confusion of the world without pushing it all the way to the kind of abstract order Yeats craved. Nor did they seek mercy from its whirling pinions; they saw its goodness in the necessity of constantly rebuilding and retooling the stories by which they understood the infinite complexity we are in.

•

And what is it that we do, we who live without cosmology, and are deluged with lifestyle fictions that say nothing of life's complexity? Let me tell you a tale of the world we inhabit:

Several years ago, in the main park of the city I live in, swans began to die under mysterious circumstances. The autopsies carried out at the local zoo soon uncovered a single cause for the deaths. The swans had died because their necks had been broken. The newspaper and television stories about the swans, accompanied always by gruesome film and photographs of the mutilated birds, received a great deal of publicity, and soon a heated public debate was taking place. What was killing the swans? What or who was the villain? A pack of marauding dogs was identified as the most likely culprit, and the SPCA and the Parks Board argued over which agency had the responsibility for capturing the dogs. While this went on, several more swans were killed. When no dogs were found, it was suggested that raccoons were responsible. Now the wildlife branch joined the

---

thrust into power by the collapse of an artificial government that had no basis for survival other than American aid. Unlike the Viet Cong, the Khmer Rouge were without a history of coherent political struggle and without a program of reconstruction. They simply did what they knew how to do.

The Vietnamese have said—belatedly and unbelievably—that the Khmer Rouge leadership consisted of crypto-fascists, puppets of the Chinese who were under orders to exterminate their own people so that China could move in Chinese nationals to crowd the Vietnamese as they have done for a thousand years. They have had nothing to say about the actions of the Khmer Rouge cadres, preferring to blame everything on Pol Pot. When I think of those cadres I just shudder.

184

struggle to elude responsibility for stopping the slaughter. And more swans died.

One evening late in the summer, a pair of lovers happened to be couched in the park near the spot where the swans congregated for the night. From their accidental and initially blissful vantage point amidst the park's lush foliage, they saw a young man approach the water's edge. The man began to speak in a soft voice to a flock of swans, throwing them scraps of bread as he spoke. Then, as they watched, spellbound as it were, the man removed his clothing, brushed back his short blond hair, and waded carefully into the water. He continued to talk to the swans in the same calm tones, and soon one bird drew close to him. He reached out his hand to stroke the sleek neck of the bird, as one might stroke a lover, and the swan bent its head to accept the caress. Then the man strangled the swan.

The couple instantly realized who the wader was, and had the presence of mind to steal his clothing. Then they ran through the park with it, half-clothed themselves, and flagged down a policeman in a patrol car. After a few minutes of questioning, the policeman accepted their story, and several more patrol cars were summoned. The swan-killer was taken into custody, pushed into the back of one of the patrol cars to the flashing pops and quiet whinings of the media cameras, which appeared as they always do, seconds after the arrest was made.

The police went through the normal scene-of-the-crime procedures. The lovers were asked several difficult questions

---

They were *Lord of the Flies* on a massive scale, the largest teenage gang in human history.

All of the explanations of the Khmer Rouge are at least partly accurate. And so are the hundreds of other theories that front or criticize the rain of American explosives and the Khmer Rouge atrocities that followed. But finally, none of the theories or explanations change the fact that the bombs and the Khmer Rouge killed an astonishing number of innocent human beings who had every right to go on living. Why are those people dead? Why aren't the right questions asked, even if there is no simple answer?

I may have the answer to that particular question. It won't be satisfactory to those who died in Cambodia, but it might lead the rest

about what they were doing in the park, and photographs were taken of the dead swan, which still floated, half-submerged, in the lagoon. The media took their own photographs of the swan, pressing close to and into the water in order to gain the most sensational possible angle. And indeed, the newspaper photograph that appeared the next day revealed small particles of a glutinous white substance floating in the water around the body of the swan.

The suspect openly, even proudly, admitted to killing the other swans. He offered no explanation for why he'd killed them, and nobody in the press or media seemed to think that an explanation was required. Crazy people are good news. Why people go crazy isn't. The man was charged with an awkward and obscure summary offence; he pleaded guilty and was convicted, and quickly committed for psychiatric observation. After three months, he was released, and is presumably somewhere on the streets right now.

•

Isn't that a dreadful anecdote? You may be asking yourself why I related it. It's really awful, filled with gratuitous violence, sexual perversion and moral turpitude, right? Did you notice that it also has highly coherent cinematic sets, some suspense, a little terror, some careful exposure of skin, and a cynical depiction of the ineptness of our public agencies? It's just like

---

of us to start asking more difficult questions. Right now, the difficult questions are getting lost because in the Global Village, explanations are all you get. And the explanations are meant to bemuse and titillate, not to produce comprehension. Comprehension creates memory, and memory has been marked for extermination.

•

Take a barely veiled scene from the Trojan War, more than three thousand years in the murky past. The Greek forces, after half a decade on the beaches of Ilium, have begun to recognize that their mission

a television drama, if you think about it. Right now, you're probably about to toss this onto the coffee table and head out to the kitchen for a snack. Diet Pepsi? Hostess Twinkies? How's your underarm deodorant holding up?

Sorry about not having a nice ending, but it's the world we live in that prevents that. We have all the information and all the sensation, but none of the stories we hear quite add up. They just pile up, a different kind of assault altogether.

---

may not be a divine one, despite Helen's beauty and divine origins. For five years these men have been at war, sometimes in pitched battles against the Trojans, but most often merely in an awkward attempt to occupy the countryside. They must exploit the peasants for food and for their sexual needs, but here they must do it with a certain care and order. Greece is far away; there are no helicopters available to fly in pizza and 7-Up from the homeland.

These Greeks are soldiers. Their job is to commit acts of violence against others. They have done their job, sometimes reluctantly, and sometimes with the barbarity allowed by war. There have been rapes and murders, even sweeps through the countryside to pacify those recalcitrant peasants who balk at providing for their needs.

After one such sweep in which a supply of Ilium's heavy red wine and several goats have been appropriated, a mixed battalion of Greeks camps out on a stretch of beach among the twisted bodies of those peasants foolish enough to have fought back. The goats are roasted over an open fire, the wine is drunk, stories of home are exchanged. They are stories of longing, mostly exaggerated tales of a domestic paradise that will never be the same for anyone around the campfire, although these men have no inkling of that. Nestor and Odysseus may sit around this campfire, braggart captains covered with sores and dreaming of an advanced technology that might end the war. That technology is still locked up in Odysseus' brain. It will come. But not just yet. Not just yet.

The Fat Family Goes to the World's Fair

Howard and I discovered the Fat Family on the train. We'd boarded at Kamloops, a small, hot and economically depressed town. It was eight in the morning, and we were bitchy and tired because the train was seven hours late and Kamloops hadn't been any kinder to us than the rest of the world had been lately. We'd spent the night in the tiny waiting room with the railroad dispatcher, a woman about forty years old who wasn't exactly getting a kick out of staying up all night on the telephone explaining why the train was late. As the hours wore on and the train got later and later, her replies to callers became shorter and louder—just loud enough, in fact, to keep us awake. After a while we gave up trying to sleep and talked to her. I don't think she appreciated having us for an audience to her irritability any more than she enjoyed talking on the phone. By the time the train finally arrived, we weren't exactly on friendly terms with her, and only barely so with one another.

The train conductor directed us to the three day coaches. We climbed on board and headed for the back coach, figuring it

---

It will appear only at the very end of the story, because the Iliad is a story about the end of a world. The Odyssey, the story that follows it, will trace the unravelling of this world, despite Penelope's best efforts. The Imperial soldiers will end their wanderings by bringing the Trojan Horse home with them, and they will turn it on their own people. Odysseus will return to slaughter the flower of the youth in his own city. The "Sackers of Cities" will turn the forces of the Imperium in upon themselves, and become landlocked and forgotten to history for more than six hundred years.

Warships off the African coast lob shells into the dense jungles of 1890. Gunboats in 1970 shell the Vietnamese jungle. An airstrike is called in to silence the harassment by mortar of partying American

189

would be the least crowded. But the second car in, there was the Fat Family. Right out of a comic strip. There was Poppa Fat, Momma Fat, Daughter-about-fourteen Fat, and Fat twelve-year-old son. Perfect demographics, except they were carrying enough excess fatty tissue to make up at least another perfect demographic family. All four of them were wearing Cleveland sports T-shirts—Browns, Indians, Cavaliers.

You couldn't miss them, not even if you were blind. They were sleeping, and they were snoring loudly, each one with a different buzz-snort-choke harmonic. They'd turned a pair of seats around and the space they'd made for themselves was so overcrowded with their fat flesh that the excess was literally oozing out into the aisle. And because they were also oozing all over one another, every few seconds an accidental nudge or kick or elbow altered the cacophony. Maybe the weirdest thing—and this was as weird a wallow as I can remember—was the Cabbage Patch dolls each of them had tucked under their arm.

I know the Fat Family sounds like a bad joke, but these people were as real as their Cabbage Patch dolls, as real as Disneyland, and on their way from Cleveland to the World's Fair. As Howard in his practical way often reminded me, I didn't make up this world. I only live in it.

•

You might be wondering why Howard and I were spending

---

troops. The strike lights up five hundred yards of green vines, then churns them into a deeper darkness. But the mortar fire doesn't stop. Not anymore.

•

In 1979, Frances Ford Coppola released a motion picture called *Apocalypse Now!*. Self-consciously made as a recapitulation of Conrad's *Heart of Darkness*, it recorded the journey of a U.S. Navy gunboat up the Mekong river into the heart of Cambodia in search of a mysterious AWOL American Special Forces colonel by the name of Kurtz. The movie's narrator, another Special Forces officer who has

the night in a small-town railroad station—or why, in the 1980s, we were taking a train in the first place. Well, we weren't there to see the sights, because there aren't any. And we weren't taking the train because we object to air travel.

We were both out of work. Howard heard that some big American corporation was hiring labourers for a mine outside Kamloops. We figured what the hell and went up. There weren't any jobs. And if there had been, we wouldn't have got them. There were at least two hundred guys like us up there all chasing the same dumb rumour.

Howard and I didn't have the right qualifications anyway. We're both in our late thirties. I've got a Masters Degree in Political Science (he calls it "Political Silence"), and he's got a number of equally unsellable degrees. Neither of us has had a good job since the Recession—Howard calls it the Depression, because it hit him harder than it did me. I've been able to wangle a series of short-term teaching jobs, but he's been scrounging work wherever he can get it. Lately the pickings have become quite a bit slimmer.

My life has been, er, okay. No complaints, really, except that I never have enough money. But I can't say I'm ever bored. When I was a teenager I discovered that just under the surface of all the bullshit and junk we all get loaded onto us, there are ideas. Hordes of ideas. Crowds, herds, flocks—too many of them to count. Jam-cans full. Most of the ideas don't make much sense, and most of them are hard to connect with what's on

---

been damaged so profoundly by his war experience that he is little more than a piece of military equipment himself, has been sent up the river to put an end to Colonel Kurtz and the blood-drenched fiefdom he has established among the Montagnard tribesmen living at the river's upper reaches. "Terminate with extreme prejudice" is the military euphemism used.

The transposition of Conrad's story to a different time and location was a peculiar one, and it succeeded only in peculiar ways. Movie-goers went to *Apocalypse Now!* expecting conventional artistic procedures—a "normal" progression of images, events, and plot. They came away intellectually and emotionally dishevelled. Some were angry, others confused, still others accepting and curious about what it was that

the surface. But God, they're exciting. They've been my life's only commanding passion ever since.

One thing I'll say for unemployment is that it's given me lots of free time to read and think. Howard feels about the same way, except that he's a little better organized than I am—even at being unemployed. Sure, every once in a while I wonder what life would have been like if neither of us had ever gotten screwed up with ideas and education. But then I think, hey, what else is there to do in life?

I haven't got a clue what I'd have been if there weren't all these ideas floating around the world. Howard says, half jokingly, that I'd have made a good undercover agent, like Kierkegaard wanted to be, or a paratrooper, because I like sneaking up on people with my latest wacky idea and landing on top of them with both feet.

I guess Howard's a little more easy-going than I am. At least he appears to be, on the surface. If I'm a born yapper, he's a born listener. And he's better at what he does than I am, I think, and every bit as obsessive about it.

Take the first time I met him. It was in graduate school. I'd bullshitted my way into a job running the university's electronic music lab, mainly so I'd be able to put my collection of jazz records on tape. Early one afternoon I came in with a stack of records under my arm, and there was Howard, freshly arrived from back East, bent over the tape console. He was so engrossed in what he was doing he didn't even look up. A Pink Floyd

---

the movie had done to them. What they saw was not art, but the one experience that transcends the chicken-hearted techniques and intentions of twentieth-century art: it was an archetypal cultural experience that galvanized and summarized its historical epoch; an intervention so powerful that it creates a bodily understanding.

The allusions and appropriations of Conrad's story pervade *Apocalypse Now!*. Some were successful, some literary and forced, and still others startlingly direct and accurate. But for all the force of the overt parallels to Conrad, the most astonishing thing about *Apocalypse Now!* is the resonances it contains from the Iliad, the Odyssey, and from nearly every great work of literature that takes fundamental world realities as its subject matter.

song was on the speakers. He was running the song, he explained distractedly, through the lab's primitive bandpass filter. That piece of information evoked a blank stare from me. I hadn't known what the gizmo was until that moment.

"I heard something in this piece," he went on. "I'm sure I heard it."

"Heard what?" I asked.

"Give me a hand," he answered," and I'll show you."

It took us six hours, but at the end of it, we'd filtered out every sound on that Pink Floyd song except the rhythm track. On the rhythm track was what Howard suspected was there: a full regalia goose-stepping Nazi march band. You could have slid that rhythm track under *Deutschland Uber Alles* without anyone noticing.

"That kind of crap is under a lot of Rock & Roll," he said. "That's what's hidden under the surface of this whole fucking world. You just have to listen carefully to hear it."

So you can see why Howard and I became friends.

•

This doesn't have much to do with the Fat Family, except that it kind of explains Howard's instant curiosity about them: he wanted to listen to them, to find what was beneath the fat exterior. For him, things are what they do, not what they're decked out to look like they're doing. People too. But he doesn't

---

I won't bore you with yet another encompassing theory of how literature works. Literature is not as important here as the job literature does, or is supposed to do. That job is to take us into those vortices where the living, the dead, and the yet-to-be-born are able to meet and converse. Most often that occurs as a descent into the underworld, as with *Heart of Darkness* and *Apocalypse Now!*.

Coppola's descent contains significant differences from its predecessors, particularly from those, like the Iliad, that document wars. There is no Trojan Horse in *Apocalyse Now!*, and no victory. Sure, Coppola's freaked-out Americans fight among themselves like the Greeks did. They're freaked out because they kill most of their enemies without ever seeing them, often more by accident and out

make a lot of nasty judgements to cover himself. Life interests him, and people interest him more than anything else: tall or short, bald or hairy, thin or, as in this case, fat. The closer he gets, the kinder his judgements are. If you can touch a person, he figures, they're probably okay.

I wasn't all that surprised, then, when Howard steered me into the empty seats across the aisle from the Fat Family.

"For Christ's sake, Howard," I complained. "We'll never get any sleep sitting next to these bozos."

Howard grinned. "Come on," he said. "I want to find out who these people are. They're interesting."

When I rolled my eyes, he went on the offensive. "Okay, smart ass. Have you seen anybody this interesting in the last twenty-four hours? Have you seen *anything* this interesting in the last ten days?"

"They're fat," I said. "And probably stupid. They've all got Cabbage Patch dolls. And they're making more noise than a truckload of lawn-mowers. That's interesting?"

"They can't be more stupid than we are, coming up here looking to become coal miners," he said. "No, really. Listen. Don't you want to find out what they've named those dolls? You could have some real fun with that."

I gave up. I tossed my duffel bag in the corner of the seat and snuggled in against it, facing the window. "I *don't* care," I said. "You can if you want to. Leave me alone so I can get some sleep."

---

of confusion and terror than by design. They are the instruments of the technology they use, not the other way around. If there is a design to their actions, they don't see it. And like Conrad's narrator in *Heart of Darkness*, the farther up the river they travel, the more convinced they are that there is no design at all.

In Coppola's movie, as in the war it depicts, the Americans were defeated because their deity—advanced technology—is ultimately indifferent to anything but its own expanded use. In the jungles of Southeast Asia, America encountered its own Stygian underworld. The movie ends there, without resolution, just as the war it depicted ended without resolution.

■

•

I tried to nod off, but I couldn't. The Fat Family was making too much noise, and Howard kept nudging me awake to look at the scenery or to talk. Okay. This is a beautiful country, no question. Mountain-filled, dotted by crystal blue subalpine lakes and yawning river gorges, like they say in the tourist brochures. But if you look more carefully, you can see how battered it is. On practically every hillside you can see the swaths of desolation where the timber has been clearcut. Mill and mining scars are everywhere you'd care to look. I suppose the rivers look okay from a distance, but I can't help remembering that they're choked up with human garbage and every other kind of filth imaginable. I've lived in this country all my life. When you live in the same place the details of it pile up and you start seeing what's really there instead of what you're told is there and important.

I guess that's why I wasn't too excited when it was announced that there was going to be a World's Fair here. A celebration, the publicity said, of communications technology and change. Just exactly which elements of communications technology and change are being celebrated wasn't made clear. Instead, they talked about how it was going to get the economy going and bring in new capital.

I don't see any great change, except that there are a lot of puffed up politicians running around holding cocktail parties

---

As a military presence, the Americans have left Southeast Asia. But the fighting is still going on, and the Khmer Rouge are still in the Cambodian jungle. The Americans took the war home with them. Now it is everywhere.

So what is it that we can see in this underworld? First, we can see that the return to tribal consciousness isn't going to work. Individual consciousness, the I/you/world split that we have operated with for three thousand years, was a response to the failure of tribal consciousness. The world grew too crowded for groupthink. As cultures began to crowd against one another, the levels of violence rose accordingly. Individual moral and political consciousness gave people the capacity to think their way through situations, to create

for themselves and people like Dolly Parton. I mean, I looked
pretty carefully at what's being done. The site is full of comic-
book technology and a lot of bright colour and a weird kind
of compulsory optimism. It's really just Disneyland—all low-
content entertainment and bullshit. The real message is *don't
you worry about a thing!*

It's a crazy world we live in. A billion dollars just so a few
politicians can get a first-hand look at Dolly Parton's melons.
I'd rather we took all that money and started fixing some of
the damage that's accumulated over the years. Howard agrees,
but he likes the Fair despite himself. He says we should repair
the world and have some fun too.

We were arguing about exactly that when a Cabbage Patch
doll dropped head first into the aisle. Howard stared at it for
a moment, then reached over and retrieved it. He turned it over
several times, somersaulting it into his lap.

"Do you know about these things?" he said, holding it up
and rapping his knuckles off its pink plastic forehead.

"I've seen them around," I answered. "This one looks like
the Fatties over there, except that its growth got stunted."

"Don't be nasty," Howard said. "Do you know about the
crazy things people are doing with them?"

"Like what?"

"Well, there's a defrocked dentist somewhere in the States
who's making a fortune putting dental braces on these things
for the kids who own them. And another company does

---

civil institutions that ameliorated the natural violence of nature, even
to run away.

Those who see the human species returning to a state of tribal
consciousness—and the proponents of the Global Village are foremost
among them—fail to recognize that every outbreak of genocide in this
century has coincided with the propagandizing of tribal consciousness.
Nazi Germany is the most obvious example. Pol Pot's Khmer
xenophobia is another.

Second, we can recognize the political history and characteristics
of mass production technology. It is always reactive and conservative.
When it becomes the cutting edge of a society, as it has become across
Western Civilization, it builds into the social, political and economic

repairs—only they call it a medical centre—and charge big bucks.''

"Seriously?''

"Yeah,'' Howard giggled. "Life insurance companies are into it, and there are adoption agencies for unwanted dolls, designer clothes, boutiques, psychiatric social workers—all kinds of crazy shit. Maybe that's what we should get into ourselves.''

"Sure,'' I said. "How?''

"Well, we could start up a resort for Cabbage Patch dolls. Print up a brochure or something. 'Cabbage Patch Lake' we'll call it. You know, sandy beaches, fun in the sun, fishing trips, mountain climbing. When the dolls arrive we toss them into a closet until the holiday is over. Then we smear a little suntan dye on them and stick them back in the mail.''

He'd let the doll drop onto the seat beside him. I picked it up, and without really thinking about what I was doing, tried to twist its head off. No luck. I started thinking about that oil exploration company that advertised that it was going to find oil on Mt. Sinai using Bible prophesy as their data base. When they were asked about geological surveys they admitted out front that finding oil there on a scientific basis was "contraindicated''. Then they said it didn't matter. They had something better— faith. They registered the company on the stock market, and all the Christian fundamentalists bid up the shares like crazy. Last I heard the stock was above five dollars a share.

"Howard,'' I said, "about a million people died of starvation

---

forms it creates, the tools and rationale for repressing intervention. These tools and rationales—the core values of the Global Village— are capable of becoming far more pervasive and powerful than the conservatism of ideologically-based societies like Russia, China or Vietnam.

Some will argue that the only force capable of intervening is a further elaboration of the same technological processes already in operation. I won't make such an argument. If that is true, then it is only a matter of time before we nuke ourselves. I'd be crazy, in that circumstance, not to tie a can to all this and spend the rest of my life trying to have a good time in the Global Village.

Anyway, I'm more frightened by something else. There is a rela-

last year. Are we nuts? We're talking about starting a holiday resort for children's dolls, and other people have actually opened up boutiques so fat farts like these can pretend that these bits of plastic have the same needs they do.''

"Maybe they do have the same needs," he giggled. "I don't know. And besides that, you and I aren't really going to do anything. We're just talking about doing it. That's why we're unemployed. The assholes who just go ahead and do it are riding around in Mercedes and stuffing white powder up their noses. This is the Dictatorship of the Entrepreneurs, remember?''

"Fuck it," I said, flipping the doll in the air and letting it fall back into the aisle. "I'd rather stay unemployed if that's all we can do.''

"That thar's Gretchen," said a voice from the ooze pile. Two beady eyes were open, the daughter's. "Dew yew lak Cabbage Patch kids?''

"They're fine," Howard answered before I could think of anything to say.

The ooze pile moved again, and a second doll landed in Howard's lap. "That's Eric," said the voice.

I still wasn't sure if it was the daughter speaking because her mouth didn't move. A third doll landed beside me, and the fourth bounced off the window. Howard caught it before it hit the floor. "That's Walt and Gladys.''

With some prodigious grunting and shoving, six more eyes appeared in the ooze. The Fat Family became relatively distinct

---

tionship between the degree of political authority being exercised and the likelihood that said authority will sooner or later embark on a policy and program of genocide. It doesn't matter what kind of authority is involved. The actions of the Khmer Rouge confirm that Marxist-Leninist governments are not excluded from this formula. Stalinism is not something created by the personality of Joseph Stalin, but a natural consequence of the practical application of Marxist-Leninist theory: The state just doesn't wither away, and the infinitely prolonged dictatorship of the proletariat creates a form of authority that naturally becomes absolute and arbitrary. The conditions in Cambodia simply led to an extreme foreshortening of the Stalinist model.

We already know that forms of political authority that attempt to

entities.

Howard was eyeing the spectacle with a grin. "Hi, there," he said.

"Hah thar yerself," said Mother Fat, assuming the role of spokesperson.

"I guess you folks are from Cleveland, eh?" he asked.

"Houston," Mother Fat corrected. "Hewsten, Tex-Ass. We were jest visitin' back in O-hi-o. Mah cousin lives in Akron. It's rill naice there, naice an' green."

"Never been there," Howard admitted. "My name's Howard."

The members of the Family introduced themselves. The kids were Gretchen and Eric, the parents Walt and Gladys.

"I see you're named after your Cabbage Patch dolls," Howard said, his grin widening to signal that he was making a joke.

"Other way round," Walt answered, blandly. "Hew's yer friend?"

I couldn't see any reason for giving my real name, so I told them I was Joseph Conrad.

"Thet's a naice name," said Gladys. "Yew related to that naice short actor who flies those old planes on TV?"

Why not, I thought. "He's my second cousin."

"No kiddin'. Isn't thet just the devil, now. And yer tall, too."

Howard changed the subject. "You folks headed for the World's Fair?"

"Wah, yes we are," Gladys said. "Is thet whar yew boys are

---

hide the connection between economic and political power, such as our own, are prone to genocide. What has never been determined (or even studied) is the point at which genocide will start. Certainly in mass societies certain kinds of external authority are necessary, if only to carry out service economies-of-scale. But there are structural reasons to distrust any and all authority, or at least to subject it to an ongoing process of interrogation.

There's nothing new in any of this except the growing power of the Global Village. The two means that human societies have found to resist the growth of authority are education and constitutional nationalism. The Global Village attacks both of those. Education—as distinct from technical training or propaganda—creates an appetite

goan?"

"We live there," Howard said before I could say no.

"Lucky boys," she replied, with an exaggerated *ooooh* in her tone. "Must be naice."

"It's a nice city," Howard said. "You'll enjoy it."

Walt straightened in his seat and reached into the ooze. "Mebbe yew can tell us a bit about what to see," he said, retrieving a small nylon bag stuffed with brochures for the Fair.

"There's some interesting exhibits," Howard said. I could see his grin twisting just a little. "But the best ones are the ones that aren't advertised well, or aren't advertised at all."

"Lak waht, for instance," Walt demanded, strewing brochures across his family's collective lap.

"Well," Howard said, his face utterly neutral, "there's the Cambodia Pavilion."

"Cambodia?" Gladys echoed. "Is thet one of those new countries in Africa? Can't recall ever hearin' of Cambodia."

"It doesn't pop up in the news much these days," Howard agreed. "It's in Asia. Near Vietnam. You remember Vietnam, don't you?"

You couldn't tell if Gladys did or didn't remember Vietnam, but Walt's complexion darkened slightly.

"Oh yeah," he said. "Had a cousin got killed thar. Hope these Cambodian fellers aren't mixed up with those Commie burners who murdered all our boys."

"They were neutral," Howard said. "They tried to be,

---

for complexity and is an obvious hindrance to the franchise consumerism that is the backbone of the Global Village. The geopolitics of mass communications—best witnessed in a country like Canada—are easily overwhelming constitutional nationalism. Loyalties are moving elsewhere, mainly to "supra-national" corporate bodies, and to their consumer images and products.

We are in an underworld, among the dead and dying of an old and moribund civilization. There are no barbarians threatening the gates of our cities, however. The barbarians are in control. Lokeshvara. Apocalyse Now. The Pepsi Generation. The place where the yet-to-be-born are being excluded.

anyway."

"Ain't no such thing as neutralness when yer fighting for a way of life," Walt said. "Yew find me somebody sittin' on the fence when the safety of the Free World and Democracy is on the line and ah'll show yew a Crypto-commie who's lookin' to get them pickets stuck straight up his ass."

"That did happen to a few Cambodians, it's true," Howard said, agreeably.

"Serves the goddamn burners right," Walt glowered.

Walt's face was getting quite red, so I changed the subject. "How come you folks didn't just go to Disneyland? It's a lot closer to home, and it's just about the same."

Happily, he was easily distracted. "Wahl," he drawled, scratching his elbow as if he were pondering something profound, "We figgered it this way. Disneyland's always bin thar and it's always goan to be thar. And yew know, this heah World's Fair is further away from whar we come from, and that's good. They say travel broadens the mind, or somethin'. So we decided to come up heah foah little look-see."

"What's Houston like?" I asked, winking at Eric so he'd know I was talking to him.

"Oh, I dinnow," the kid answered in an accent thicker than the others. "We live innah subub. Watcha lota TV. It's rill hot thar, yinnow. Same's anyplace, ah guess, but rill hot, yinnow?"

Walt interrupted. "This heah Cambodia Pavilion," he said, pulling open a site map of the Fair. "Now whar the hell kin

---

11

Let the new story begin right here, with the New People of the Global Village, in the face of Lokeshvara, the grinning Bodhisattva that communicates everything and knows nothing. But where am I? If this is the Stanleyville Station or the humid jungle of Cambodia it doesn't act like it.

There is a woman sitting at the table next to me. She's attractive, artificially blonde and about forty years old. I know roughly what she's doing, but nothing of who she is and what she thinks about the world around her. She's working up an elaborate schedule of her upcoming activities on preprinted sheets. She's an aerobics instructor, and she's

we find that on heah?"

I could almost hear Howard's mind revving up as he took the map from Walt. He pored over it, tracing his finger back and forth from the index to the graphic. "Isn't that a son-of-a-bitch?" he said. "It isn't on here."

"That's deliberate," I said. "They decided to turn it into a puzzle—make it a little more fun—so they turned it into the mystery pavilion, sort of. You have to find it for yourself, without a guide or a map."

Howard was gazing at me appreciatively. Walt and the rest of the Fat Family just looked bemused.

"That's right," he echoed. "Now I remember. I heard they even change the location, and so on. When somebody finds the pavilion, they get a special prize."

"Oh yeah?" Eric said, his face breaking into a grin that almost submerged his eyes. "Thas neat. Wassa prize?"

"Nobody who finds the pavilion tells what the prize is," I said. "That's part of the mystery, I guess. You only understand it if you find the pavilion, and afterward you don't talk about it. But I've heard that once you find it, you get a lot more out of the rest of the fair than you would if you didn't."

Walt snorted approvingly. "My god, what they goan think of next? Must be lak one of those VIP passes, so's you kin just walk inta the rest of the Fair without waiting. We'll havta look for that Cambodia Pavilion rill hard."

"Les go eat, Poppa," Gretchen said. "Dining cah must be

---

scheduling her body through the next week: so many calories a day, so many situps, squat-thrusts, so many hours jiggling and jumping to canned Rock & Roll. I wonder how many thoughts she has scheduled.

There's nothing funny about this woman. She isn't going to read this book when it comes out, and I know why. Too negative. And anyhow, she reads infrequently. Stephen King, maybe, but they turn all his books into movies, don't they? She'll wait for the video release and rent it to watch on her home VCR. You can't read books while you're doing aerobics.

Get serious, you say.

Fine. This is not a dark place. Nobody is being killed here. Most

open bah now."

The Fat Family forgot all about the Cambodia Pavilion and us at the suggestion of food. They began the tricky task of re-arranging themselves so they could exit from their wallow. When Walt stood up, I swear the coach almost derailed. Gretchen gestured to me for her Cabbage Patch doll, and I surrendered it.

"Dew yew wanna come 'long fer some brekkie or stay heah with these boys?" She asked it, snub-nose to snub-nose.

The doll didn't answer, but Gladys did. "Gretchen's tryin' to lose weight," she said. "Leave huh heah."

"See?" Howard demanded as they disappeared into the next car.

"See what?" I said. "All I see is four fat slugs going off to stuff their faces."

"No," he said. "They're going to wander all over the World's Fair demanding to be told where the Cambodia Pavilion is. And they won't believe there isn't one."

"So what? All that will produce is more wacko Disneyland. They won't look out of place at all."

"No, you dope. They'll *be* the Cambodia Pavilion."

"Fuck off," I said. "It's one thing to string along some unsuspecting tourists. But you and I have got to remember that there is no Cambodia Pavilion. There's no Cambodia, period. They're Kampucheans now. They wiped out millions of their own people, and our memory of that has been wiped out by crap like the World's Fair. If anyone was serious about what

---

of the people I know have never witnessed a death closer to their own lives than that of a domestic animal, or of a swallow that flies into a picture window and breaks its neck. Right outside here people feed the pigeons and ducks, and engage in other acts of simple kindness. Yet most of these people, including myself, are frightened. Is my house being broken into? Will we be nuked in the near future? Is it safe to speak to strangers? Is it safe to be touched by another human being?

As a writer I have a couple of additional fears: if I discover the truth, can I tell it? Will anyone listen, and if they do are they equipped to care or to act upon it?

Yes, this is a pleasant place. Its pleasures make it hard to see that most of the humane achievements of the past forty years are being

happened in Cambodia they would put up a pavilion for all the Cambodians who were murdered, and they'd show how the ideology and the foreign policy worked, theirs and ours, and they'd show examples of the technology used, and they'd show what it did. They'd cover the pavilion with human skulls—real ones.''

"No," Howard said, the pleasure of the gag completely gone. "That wouldn't be allowed. It's in bad taste. Don't even fantasize about it. Look at the Fat Family for what it is. They're reasonably nice people, right? But you look at Walt, and he's not just fat old Walt. He's this thing in all of us that's devouring the world. In a way, Walt's the Cambodia Pavilion. Him and God knows how many others who come to the Fair to experience all that fake joy the Fair cooks up for them.''

"That's pretty humourless of you. Being humourless is supposed to be my job. And anyway, I'm not sure I get it. Walt's the opposite of Cambodia.''

"No, he isn't. You're wrong about something else too. You said that nobody could remember what happened in Cambodia, but that's not true. Not every memory has been erased. My memory works okay, and so does yours. Lots of people have memories that work. We're still alive, and we're still thinking.''

"Yeah," I said. "Maybe. But maybe these technological systems are stronger than our memories. Maybe they're going to replace memory. Maybe they're the next phase in the evolution of being. Maybe while we're sitting here believing

---

eroded by the inability to forego those pleasures, and by the growth of uncontrolled authority.

A group of anarchists blow up a power station. They are swiftly caught, the power station is rebuilt, and the government forms a special three hundred member anti-terrorist organization to aid the police in detecting the next anarchist group before it can strike.

In the schools, a witch hunt is going on. A teacher, somewhere in the past, molested several children. The culprit is exposed and jailed, but the media's handling of the trial has made a potential child molester out of every teacher. The teachers respond with a public statement declaring their unwillingness to touch their students.

AIDS makes all casual sexual contact potentially lethal, and other

that we're the pinnacle of life's complexity, we should remember that amoebas were pinnacles of complexity once."

"Okay," Howard said. "That's a possibility. And if it's true, there's not a goddamned thing any of us can do about it. So why worry about it?" He stifled a giggle, then let it come out. "That's just like you to appeal to science fiction when you're losing an argument. That way you can continue to whine and bitch, instead of figuring it out to have more fun with what's there."

"Pretty macabre fun we're having here," I said.

"It's not so bad," he said. "We're human beings. We're weird."

•

So, that's more or less the story of the Fat Family, or as much of it as I know. I mean, they did come back from breakfast eventually, the train didn't derail, and we all got to our destination alive and well. Howard and I even walked with them over to the gates of the Fair. That was the last I saw of them.

I wish it was the last I heard or saw of the Cambodia Pavilion. One of the strange things about ideas is that they have a life of their own. They take over people and sometimes whole countries. The idea of the Cambodia Pavilion kind of did that to Howard.

About a week after we got back, he got a job on the Fair site,

---

viruses make intimate contact a danger to health. Slick television evangelists in three-piece suits smugly declare the viruses a divine plague and demand money for salvation, offering direct experience with Jesus and personal salvation without the necessity of moral stricture, discipline or action of any kind except donations to the evangelist's organization. They'll even send you some literature.

Every explanation isolates us, here. Every answer is an authoritarian one. Let the Government do it. Let Big Business do it. Unleash the entrepreneurial spirit. And soon, no one to ask the questions.

•

working as a clown of some sort. I don't know what he was doing—making people jolly, I guess, like everyone else working there. I didn't go down, and he never quite got around to explaining what it was he did to make them jolly. Last time I saw him I kidded him about the Fat Family, saying he was down there helping them find the Cambodia Pavilion.

"Nah," he said with a perfectly straight face, "I'm too busy celebrating to help anyone look for it."

"Celebrating what?"

"No one knows," he said. "No one seems to care. You go down there and it's party time. The place is up against you so tight you don't get to ask questions like that."

"Sounds kind of scary," I said. "Think I'll stay clear."

"Yeah," he said, more serious now. "It is frightening. It's like one of those festivals they held in the Middle Ages where they celebrated the plague."

"They weren't celebrating the plague," I corrected. "They were celebrating having survived the plague."

Howard stared right past me. "That's what I used to think," he said. "But I've changed my mind. I think they were celebrating the end of the world."

"Well," I said, "Don't get paranoid."

"I can't help myself," Howard said. "I can't talk to anyone—not really, and I can't hear anyone. It really is like the end of the world down there."

"Christ, Howard," I said. "Snap out of it. If it's that horrible,

---

Explain this one to yourself. A Cambodian refugee told an American writer that when the Khmer Rouge made the decision to execute a family, they carried it out in the following order: The children were killed first, youngest to oldest if there was more than one child. Then the parents were killed, wife first, then husband. If there were grandparents, they died last. They did it in this order because they wanted to exact the greatest possible degree of suffering from the victims, and because they wanted to humiliate the most basic social unit of humanity. Like so many of brutal Khmer Rouge practices, this one was an attack on memory.

I find myself remembering one of Prince Sihanouk's objections to the behaviour of the Khmer Rouge. He said that the Khmer Rouge

206

you'd better quit.''

"I can't," he said, flatly. There was a long silence. "I'm making the Cambodia Pavilion. Building it.''

•

I wish I could have that conversation with him over again. I wouldn't have let it end like that. But I did. And several weeks later Howard killed himself.

Sorry to be so abrupt. I know it doesn't quite make sense. But there you are. Or rather, here I am. I talk about Howard in the present tense because I refuse to believe he's gone. I'd like to have the courage to go down there and figure out what it was that did it to him. Maybe I'd find the Cambodia Pavilion for myself. And maybe I'd find the Fat Family with their Cabbage Patch dolls, wandering through the bright colours with blank smiles on their faces, celebrating whatever it is we all seem to be celebrating these days.

---

withheld the basic human right to be loved. At the time that I read it, his objection seemed almost quaint. To demand the right to be loved when hundreds of thousands of people were being suffocated with disposable plastic bags struck me as the objection of someone who does not understand political reality.

But perhaps Sihanouk was right. Basic human rights should be that direct and simple-minded: to have the right to walk in a park in the early morning; to have the right to grow tomatoes next to one's doorstep; to have the right to listen to the night breezes in the trees; to have the right to know what the night breezes carry.

To have the right to remember the past and to have the right to imagine a future.

Brian Fawcett was born in Prince George, British Columbia. He was graduated from Simon Fraser University in Vancouver, B.C., where he now lives "on the periphery of the Imperium." He worked for many years as a community organizer and urban planner until he began writing full time. Three collections of his short stories have been published in Canada and his poetry has been anthologized in the *Oxford Book of Canadian Poets*. In addition to his writing, Fawcett lectures widely and has taught creative writing in maximum security prisons.